Carla van Dam, PhD

The Socially Skilled Child Molester
Differentiating the Guilty from the Falsely Accused

*Pre-publication
REVIEWS,
COMMENTARIES,
EVALUATIONS . . .*

"*The Socially Skilled Child Molester* provides a thorough description of common types of child molesters, most importantly distinguishing between 'grabbers' and 'groomers'. Several common patterns of groomers are identified based on composites of interviews with thousands of child molesters. The book identifies common patterns of inappropriate behavior by abusers that are often overlooked, minimized, explained away, or seen in isolation. The book offers clear descriptions of common worrisome behaviors, common inadequate community responses, ways to break through the denial of 'it can't happen here' or 'but he was so nice,' and identifies more effective ways for adults to protect the children in their communities and stop child sexual abuse from going undetected. Common patterns of defense by child molesters are also identified and help to distinguish between molesters and those falsely accused. This book could be helpful to anyone interested in stopping child sexual abuse, correctly identifying potential perpetrators, and more accurately predicting risk of re-offending."

Kelly Simonson, PhD
Licensed Psychologist,
Texas Woman's University
Counseling Center

More pre-publication
REVIEWS, COMMENTARIES, EVALUATIONS . . .

"**A** provocative analysis of four types of smarter, richer, socially skilled, and often litigious offenders as opposed to the cruder, more frequently captured types. Such offenders, whom the author calls 'groomers,' usually spend more time cultivating the good graces of family members, neighborhoods, and whole communities rather than selecting and seducing their victims. These are offenders usually regarded as upstanding pillars of the community, and include businessmen, priests, judges, coaches, teachers, and volunteers. The book offers unique criminological insights into the mindsets of empowered, enabled offenders. Perhaps most importantly, it also sheds light on exactly what communities can do to become more vigilant. The typology is well-developed and each type of offender is extensively discussed in jargon-free fashion. Criminologists and forensic psychologists will probably find the chapters on interviewing protocols and risk assessment instruments most useful, but the average reader can certainly benefit from this book as well."

Thomas R. O'Connor, PhD
Associate Professor of Justice Studies
& Applied Criminology,
North Carolina Wesleyan College

"**T**his book is one of the most important treatises published on the identification of the child molester I call the 'three-piece suiter.' Carla van Dam carefully describes the various child molesters who sit next to us in our churches and synagogues, go to the theater, and eat in the same restaurants with us. They continue to harm children because they fool us into thinking that such nice guys couldn't do such a terrible thing. But they do. Read this book and memorize who they are, and you will be protecting children."

Lenore E. Walker, EdD
Author of *The Battered Woman,*
The Battered Woman Syndrome, Handbook of Child Sexual Abuse, and *Abused Women & Survivor Therapy;*
Professor of Psychology
and Coordinator of Forensic
Psychology Concentration, Nova
Southeastern University

"**C**arla van Dam shines a cold and clear light on the murky depths of child molesters and how they perpetrate their offences so often without getting caught. This book's graphic details, drawn from thousands of cases, will help everyone who has to deal with widespread problems do so more intelligently and effectively."

Professor David Canter, PhD
Director of the Centre for Investigative
Psychology, The University of Liverpool,
United Kingdom

"**T**his is the most complete book I have read relating to child molesters. Carla van Dam has written it in such a way that professionals in the field as well as general readers can understand and learn. This should be required reading for anyone in law enforcement."

Steve Thompson, MS
Associate Professor and Sexual
Aggression Services Coordinator,
Central Michigan University

The Socially Skilled Child Molester

Differentiating the Guilty from the Falsely Accused

The Haworth Press
Titles of Related Interest

The Socially Skilled Child Molester
Differentiating the Guilty from the Falsely Accused

Carla van Dam, PhD

The Haworth Press®
New York • London • Oxford

For more information on this book or to order, visit
http://www.haworthpress.com/store/product.asp?sku=5524

or call 1-800-HAWORTH (800-429-6784) in the United States and Canada
or (607) 722-5857 outside the United States and Canada

or contact orders@HaworthPress.com

Published by

The Haworth Press, Inc., 10 Alice Street, Binghamton, NY 13904-1580.

PUBLISHER'S NOTES
The development, preparation, and publication of this work has been undertaken with great care. However, the Publisher, employees, editors, and agents of The Haworth Press are not responsible for any errors contained herein or for consequences that may ensue from use of materials or information contained in this work. The Haworth Press is committed to the dissemination of ideas and information according to the highest standards of intellectual freedom and the free exchange of ideas. Statements made and opinions expressed in this publication do not necessarily reflect the views of the Publisher, Directors, management, or staff of The Haworth Press, Inc., or an endorsement by them.

Case studies in this book are composites based on thousands of interviews. Any resemblance to actual persons, living or dead, is entirely coincidental.

Cover design by Jennifer M. Gaska.

Library of Congress Cataloging-in-Publication Data

van Dam, Carla, 1950-
    The socially skilled child molester: differentiating the guilty from the falsely accused / Carla van Dam.
       p. cm.
    Includes bibliographical references and index.
    ISBN-13: 978-0-7890-2805-1 (hard : alk. paper)
    ISBN-10: 0-7890-2805-0 (hard : alk. paper)
    ISBN-13: 978-0-7890-2806-8 (soft : alk. paper)
    ISBN-10: 0-7890-2806-9 (soft : alk. paper)
    1. Child molesters—Psychology. 2. Criminal behavior, Prediction of. 3. Child sexual abuse—Prevention. I. Title.
HV6570.V36 2006
616.85'836—dc22

2005018236

CONTENTS

Preface

Socially skilled child molesters use predictable strategies to ingratiate themselves into communities in order to abuse children. By unmasking their operating techniques, the differences between those who molest and those who do not can become visible. This book provides all adults responsible for protecting children with the necessary tools to make the invisible visible and collaborate meaningfully to stop child molesters.

ABOUT THE AUTHOR

Carla van Dam, PhD, is a clinical and forensic psychologist who has practiced in both the United States and Canada, and has taught at several universities. Her focus has been on developing a balanced approach to protecting communities by better understanding those who sexually molest children. In addition to extensive forensic work and innumerable evaluations on known child molesters, she has trained professionals, done public speaking, worked with the legal system, consulted with various organizations, and helped community groups manage this complicated terrain. Past publications include journal articles, a first aid manual for helping those who have been molested, and a book on how to stop providing potential molesters with access to children titled *Identifying Child Molesters: Preventing Child Sexual Abuse by Recognizing the Patterns of the Offenders* (Haworth). For the past twenty-five years Dr. van Dam has focused on primary prevention strategies to help end child sexual abuse.

Acknowledgments

This book would not have been possible without the help of many different people. Ongoing appreciation goes to my mother. Her support, loyalty, and strength of character are an inspiration. Special thanks to Roger Wolfe, a pioneer who has been steadfast in setting admirable standards and maintaining integrity in this field. Sincere thanks go to Chuck Bates, PhD, for his ongoing willingness to discuss the ideas presented in this book and his cheerful continued help in clarifying, fine-tuning, and editing the material presented here. Without his assistance, this book would never have been possible. Ongoing appreciation goes to Linda Halliday-Sumner, who originally introduced the topic to me in 1980, and who has enacted many of the ideas presented here, thereby demonstrating the importance of empowering those who have been molested. Thanks also go to a number of colleagues for their editorial assistance and mentoring, including Iris E.V. Rucker, PhD, and Jan Lewis, PhD. I am also grateful for the initial editorial assistance provided by The Haworth Press' Editor Bob Geffner, PhD, and the superb copyediting done by Mary Beth Madden of The Haworth Press. A number of other people have helped fine-tune this project through their knowledge of community concerns and their experiences with the dilemmas faced by those encountering the challenges created wherever child sexual abuse occurs. Thanks also go to Mary Anne Harrington, as well as to Laina Berry for coining the name "Marvelous Marvin." Most of all, this project has been made possible by the hundreds of people who shared their personal experiences and who have shouldered the onerous task of trying to protect children against overwhelmingly complex obstacles.

Introduction

This book is intended to identify the habits of socially skilled child molesters, referred to in this book as "Groomers," who successfully ingratiate themselves into the hearts and homes of adults in order to sexually assault children with impunity. Their habits are so predictable, their activities so constant, and the harm they cause so extensive, society cannot afford to continue inadvertently enabling their misconduct. They are responsible for most child sexual abuse cases, yet can only be stopped when communities become trained and educated to recognize the problem, know what to do, and collaborate meaningfully to make the world less safe for child molesters. Communities that correctly recognize the grooming patterns of these molesters will have children who are less vulnerable to abuse.

To stop these socially skilled child molesters, adults need to ensure that the clues seen in isolation by various community members become known rather than remaining invisible or compartmentalized. Molesters, whose manipulative manners charm or intimidate adults into believing them to be above reproach, can often be identified by those familiar with their stereotyped operating methods. While socially skilled child molesters continue to successfully target whole communities, often molesting hundreds of children without being stopped, educated adults can make entire communities unsafe for them. This can be done by empowering victims, and collaborating effectively with community members to ensure that all relevant information is incorporated into investigations, thereby sending a clear message that preying on children will not be tolerated.

Identifying their methods and recognizing the danger they present will be done through a number of case studies that let the reader see exactly how they operate. Recommendations are then made on how to stop giving these molesters access to children.

The book is organized into ten chapters outlined as follows:

Chapter 1, "Understanding the Problem": This chapter focuses on recognizing that the well-socialized child molesters, namely the Groomers described in this book, behave as if they were addicted to having sex with children. Understanding this is crucial to improving prevention and intervention strategies. Recognizing the addictive nature of their conduct also becomes a necessary underlying component to more effectively investigating the cases and more appropriately managing community safety precisely because the behavior is much more frequent than would be readily visible to those relying only on conviction data to ascertain risk.

Chapter 2, "Child Molesters in Their Natural Habitat": In this chapter a number of representative cases help familiarize the reader with the operating styles of the well-socialized child molesters. Becoming familiar with the often predictable practices of the Groomers under study creates the framework for more effectively preventing child sexual abuse, as well as intervening earlier in child sexual abuse cases.

This chapter introduces the reader to a number of child molesters to see how they typically operate. Such firsthand information reveals why they are so successful, and builds the foundation for changing management and safety practices.

This book is based on information from innumerable cases representing child molesters who successfully operate in every community. Readers unfamiliar with the more sordid aspects of child sexual abuse may find these stories both unbelievable and unsettling. Even those professionals who work with the victims of child sexual abuse and the families of these victims often lack detailed information on how the child molesters operate, information crucial to working more effectively. Many of the cases in this book are composites based on thousands of interviews with child molesters. These individuals will be referred to by first names only to remind the reader that they are composite cases. Relying on composite cases was done because the information revealed in the thousands of interviews with offenders, with various family members, and with community groups was consistent. Composite profiles, therefore, are seen as a more efficient method to convey the information.

A few stories provided in this book refer to specific offenders. Because the cases are a matter of public record, these offenders are named. The reader should be warned, however, that the composite cases are as real as the information revolving around named offenders, and the composite cases should not be perceived as being fictional. The consistency of the practices and strategies of the well-socialized Groomers being examined in this book are successful because of continued public ignorance. Recognizing their operating methods is essential to unmasking them.

The reader will learn of four composite cases whose stories are clichés: Bold Businessman Bob, Marvelous Moving Marvin, Cranky Coach Carl, and Divine Dr. Dan. Bottom-feeder Buddy will also be introduced to show that not all the child molesters under discussion are equally sophisticated. Their stories will be referred to throughout the book to exemplify the concealed operating strategies of the Groomers.

Chapter 3, "Current Practices": This chapter provides the reader with information on how child sexual abuse is currently addressed, and how Groomers are now managed by the community and the legal system. This is essential to showing how the inadequacies of current practices spring from key misapprehensions of the Groomer phenomenon. Eliminating child sexual abuse requires additional prevention and intervention strategies that can only happen once everyone becomes familiar with the true dynamics of child sexual abuse.

Chapter 4, "Not All Child Molesters Are Alike": This chapter presents a closer focus on the vocabulary used to describe sexual misconduct to provide greater clarification for examining various kinds of risk. Much of the damage to children results from child molesters who first carefully groom adults in order to gain access to children. This chapter extends and deepens the understanding needed to recognize this Groomer profile to correctly differentiate Groomers from Grabbers.

Chapter 5, "Common Misperceptions": This chapter addresses how current practices allow behaviors and stories often used by the Groomers to be excused. Such events are often misunderstood, too frequently ignored, or even accepted. Groomer excuses and explanations, when their conduct is challenged, are hackneyed clichés that are often misconstrued as sincere. Everyone needs to know them well enough to recognize them when they occur.

Chapter 6, "Accurately Differentiating Danger": This chapter will provide the framework to understand how the behaviors of those who are Groomers often vary from those whose conduct should not be considered worrisome. Unfortunately, innocent individuals are sometimes falsely accused of being child molesters. Behavioral patterns of successful Groomers frequently vary significantly from those who are not child molesters. An informed investigation will usually reveal these differences. Managing such an investigation requires knowing what to look for and where to look. This chapter helps the reader differentiate the Groomer child molester from someone whose behavior should not be considered suspect.

Much as one can tell where a slug has been by following the trail of slime, those who are truly guilty of sexually molesting children typically leave a slime trail of evidence. Understanding how to follow that trail will be further accomplished through additional case studies utilized throughout the rest of the book to help the reader learn to better recognize the behavior habits of Groomers as well as to compare them to individuals whose behavior is not dangerous. Again, some of the cases used will be composites.

The reader will see Predictable Peter, finally unmasked after fifty years of sex-offending conduct, whose addictive behavior represents the patterns typically seen among Groomers. On the other hand, both Truthful Tim and Innocent Isaac are cases based on innocent people mistakenly caught in the pedophile dragnet. Although Innocent Isaac is labeled a child molester because his girlfriend is underage, Gary Little's story reveals how a careful operator can use those same legal limits to his advantage, successfully molesting hundreds of boys, and using his knowledge of the law to skirt legal danger while using his position of power to access victims. The story of Helpful Harry will allow the reader to better differentiate between the helpfulness of the kind-hearted person as opposed to the manipulative assistance such Groomers as Slippery Sam use, thereby further revealing the Groomer Profile.

Chapter 7, "A Framework for Understanding Child Sexual Abuse": In this chapter, the iceberg is provided as an illustration to reveal not just the tip, but the "underwater" data as well. Revealing the iceberg in its entirety includes more of what is actually known about child molester behavior by those who encounter them, evidence that rarely becomes officially identified but should be incorporated in decision making and risk management planning. In other words, rather than merely looking at the tip of the iceberg, this framework provides an underwater exposure of the larger body of evidence that revolves around the phenomenon of the Groomers' operating strategies responsible for most child sexual abuse. Understanding this framework is essential to making necessary changes for more effectively protecting children.

Chapter 8, "Interviewing Child Molesters": This chapter helps the reader understand that despite the fact that the grooming child molesters under study are incredibly successful liars, the lies they tell can be identified. In fact, their explanations and their strategies are often predictable. Becoming familiar with these patterns will allow the reader to know that such stories should ring alarm bells and suggest the need for closer scrutiny. By learning to listen carefully, knowing the questions to ask, and paying close attention to the discrepancies and inconsistencies, those who encounter child molesters in their homes and communities or work with them professionally will be less gullible.

Chapter 9, "Predicting Risk": This chapter examines current practices used for determining continued risk of known child molesters. These methods are more closely examined within the context of how the Groomers operate, utilizing the framework introduced in Chapter 7, and delineating how much of the behavior associated with child sexual abuse typically remains invisible to the authorities. Tools currently used to differentiate convicted offenders who are dangerous from less dangerous individuals rely on evidence that fails to incorporate the rich qualitative information known by those who live with the offenders. This information is necessary to more thoroughly understand the dilemma, more effectively manage the offenders, and more accurately predict the risk for further danger.

Chapter 10, "Incorporating Corroborating Evidence": This chapter will help the reader chart a course of action by reviewing principles offered in the previous chapters. It provides strategies that can be used by investigators to better access the information about known child molesters, and includes a proposal for making the public's knowledge more readily available to the authorities. Community networking is necessary to help everyone gain access to all the pieces of the puzzle that are crucial for protecting children. Such knowledge is essential for investigating cases and should be incorporated into treatment planning. Knowledge is important to determining management guidelines, and is required to more accurately assess ongoing risk.

Finally, each sexual abuse victim holds the key to ending the abuse of others. Their information can correctly identify offenders whose conduct need not be protected, tolerated, or supported. By working together with clarity and support, they can help reveal what is truly below the tip of the iceberg.

Chapter 1

Understanding the Problem

CHILD MOLESTERS AS ADDICTS

To more effectively stop children from ever being abused means better understanding child molesters, recognizing how they operate, and learning how they think and feel. The kinds of child molesters described in this book, those who commit most of the sexual assaults against children (Salter, 2003; Bolen, 2001), behave as sexual addicts who continuously fantasize about having sex with children, are sexually aroused to children, and enjoy getting away with it (Carnes, 1983, 1996; Flora, 2001). Viewing their compulsive behavior as being like an addiction, in this case being addicted to having sex with children, in the same manner as one would view heroin addicts who are addicted to heroin, helps provide a framework to more accurately understand the behavior. Those familiar with addictions recognize that the addiction drives the behavior because every act is directed at obtaining greater access to the drug of choice. For that reason, addicts primarily associate with people who can help them facilitate that goal, and do not tolerate those who interfere with that goal. The child molesters described in this book similarly primarily associate with adults who can provide them with access to children, or who can help them polish their image with parents so they can have access to children.

The child molesters described in this book are no different from any other addict, but in this case everything about their behavior is ruled by their desire to have sex with children; every encounter with adults facilitates that goal. Every activity is designed to get better access to children. The smarter, richer, more socially skilled these child molesters, the greater success they experience. The addictive nature of their behavior ensures that they continuously engage in activities to access children, to molest children, and to avoid getting caught.

This is what offenders reveal when assured clemency (Abel, Rouleau, & Cunnhingham-Rathner, 1986), when unmasked (The Investigative Staff of *The Boston Globe,* 2002), when boasting (Silva, 1990), or when confessing past conduct (Cook, 1989). Convicted child molesters rarely share their "trade secrets" with outsiders, yet when they do, they often report molesting hundreds of victims over their careers (Bolen, 2001).

That is why the child molesters described in this book, the socially skilled, respected, or feared individuals, are always on task, namely looking for opportunities to have sex with children. Their image management serves to give them access to children. Their good deeds are meant to get them closer to children. Their constant activities, leaving them almost no personal time, are geared toward accessing victims. Ingratiating themselves with the adults and doing damage control are all necessary to provide ongoing repeated opportunities to have sex with children.

The reasons these molesters so frequently succeed at sexually molesting children is described in this book. The people responsible for protecting children are sometimes enchanted by the smooth talk, friendly action, and kind support Groomers provide. Parents are typically so successfully co-opted by the offender that when they become even slightly suspicious, they typically worry about ruining the reputations of respectable citizens, or being sued. They therefore usually decide to keep quiet, look more carefully, or wait for clearer information.

The people responsible for protecting children also often find the topic shameful, embarrassing, and frightening. As a result, they frequently keep quiet and assume whatever happens to be their fault, a one-time error in judgment, or a misunderstanding. However, their very embarrassment and discomfort with the topic helps foster a willingness to accept lame excuses from the molester. Furthermore, because they cannot fathom that people they know and love could be child molesters, assuming child molesters to be "street scum" rather than respectable people who masquerade a genuine interest in children, they incorrectly presume "it can't happen here," thereby making themselves more vulnerable to attack.

Those parents who do believe their children are being abused often doubt the suspected molester would do this to anyone else. As a result, they privately endure their dilemma, sure no one else could be similarly harmed. They are also more readily intimidated into silence and secrecy because they feel isolated. Attempts to stop the molester are easily ended, because when challenged or cornered, these molesters typically go on the offensive, threatening to sue for slander, and making accusations of malice anytime someone threatens access to the addictive sexual contact they crave (Millon, Simonsen, Birket-Smith, & Davis, 1998). Timid adults usually back off when confronted by these masterful confident Groomers who become righteously indignant.

Child molesters also gravitate to those people who are most likely to be too polite to fend them off, too shy and anxious to tell them to leave, too dependent to be assertive, and too impressed by rank, power, status, or money to do the right thing. Child molesters deliberately associate with adults who cannot address these issues. They seek out adults who worry about hurting people's feelings. They charm adults who do not believe it could happen.

In other words, the children most at risk of being sexually abused by these Groomers are the children surrounded by adults who cannot stomach learning about child sexual abuse. These adults may therefore inadvertently be more likely to welcome child molesters into their homes, organizations, or communities, ignore the evidence, overcome concerns, and talk themselves out of believing possible suspicions. Adults who are timid, shy, obedient, and polite, and who ignore suspicious discrepancies for fear of hurting the feelings of child molesters, are unaware that these characteristics are more likely to make them lightning rods for Groomers.

Child molesters who are addicted to having sex with children are therefore more likely to appear wherever children congregate. They choose careers and hobbies that give them access to children. They become coaches, educators, therapists, child-care workers, babysitters, priests, ministers, hospice care providers, and pediatricians. They marry into families with children. The list of opportunities to gain access to children is endless. This does not mean all coaches, educators, therapists, child-care workers, babysitters, priests, ministers, hospice care providers, or pediatricians are child molesters. Rather, the reverse is true. Child molesters rely on these and other opportunities to access children.

Child molesters are continuously busy with activities to gain access to children, but they focus on children only after the adults responsible for those children have signaled an unwillingness to monitor boundary violations, thereby having communicated that subtle cues of misconduct will be overlooked, ignored, or tolerated (van Dam, 2001). Groomers test this hypothesis by pushing boundaries of privacy, personal space, and touching of children in front of the adults, while carefully monitoring the reactions of surrounding adults. The Groomers look for those adults who seem oblivious to improprieties, do nothing, or say nothing, because they know those adults are the key gatekeepers for safe access to children. The Groomers then know those are the children to molest.

Groomers do not waste time with children when adults do not exhibit codependent passivity or inattention. Adults who understand these dynamics, trust their instincts, do not tolerate improprieties, are assertive, and clearly set boundaries tend to be avoided because they cannot be safely manipulated, and their children are most likely to tell. These Groomers know better than to waste their time around such families or communities, as time spent with people who cannot deliver victims is time stolen from the Groomer's "raison d'être."

SEXUAL DEPENDENCE

Mental health professionals rely on the *Diagnostic and Statistical Manual of Mental Disorders,* Fourth Edition, Text Revision (DSM-IV TR) (APA, 2000) as the authority in distinguishing between addictions and lesser problems easily corrected with information and motivation. Addictions, as noted by the DSM-IV TR, are different from compulsive behaviors, which tend to more consistently occur to moderate anxiety (Schwartz & Begley, 2002; APA, 2000). Criteria for meeting the diagnosis of substance dependence is clearly delineated for clinicians. The sexual molesters under discussion meet the criteria for dependency, in this case their drug of choice being sex with children. With only a slight alteration in the wording, the criteria used for determining substance dependence could also be used to describe the addictive sexual nature of the offenders under discussion. Namely, the Groomers who exhibit three of the following behaviors would meet criteria for their sexual misconduct to be viewed as an addiction:

- preoccupied with sexual interactions with children
- need for sex with children escalates in frequency and/or intensity
- unsuccessful in controlling the behavior
- irritable when trying to control the behavior

- uses sex with children to escape from problems or relieve dysphoria
- returns to sexual activities despite incarceration or almost being caught
- lies to others to mask sexual activities with children
- jeopardizes community standing to maintain sexual contact with children

Viewing these offenders as meeting criteria for sexual dependence is not in lieu of the DSM-IV TR criteria for the diagnosis of pedophilia, but rather an expansion to more specifically recognize that these prolific Grooming child molesters behave as if they were sexual addicts. This perspective is particularly useful for better protecting children from the type of molesters under discussion, precisely because the addictive nature of their behavior will help better direct investigations, guide reporting strategies, and develop monitoring recommendations.

Chapter 2

Child Molesters in Their Natural Habitat

The problem with child sexual abuse is that most people do not understand the nature of the beast, and find the topic too distasteful. They would rather not know. Unfortunately, ignorance is not bliss, but an invitation for children to be preyed upon. Just as adults who learn basic first-aid strategies despite discomfort with blood and gore are able to help save lives, people who face the sleazy repugnant facts about how child molesters operate, and are willing to consider the possibility that these offenders exist in every community, are positioned to render whole neighborhoods safer from child sexual abuse.

This book focuses on the prevention and intervention strategies for stopping those offenders who carefully select victims they already know. These are the "Groomers" who first ingratiate themselves with adults for the express purpose of being given free access to children by innocent but ignorant adults. Only a very small percentage of child molesters are the "Grabbers" who attack strangers (Bolen, 2001). Such "stranger danger" requires other prevention strategies not addressed in this book. Rather, the focus here is on the majority of cases, namely those molesters who have first deliberately ingratiated themselves with the adult community. They groom the parents, school, church, sports club, or any other organization where children congregate, into accepting them as upstanding citizens in the community. These child molesters are known, loved, trusted, or possibly feared, and their conduct is, unfortunately, assumed to be "above reproach." As a result, these offenders obtain continued free access to victims by the very adults responsible for protecting children.

Although the information in this book consistently refers to child molesters as being males, women are also known to sexually molest children. Some of the strategies that women use are similar to the techniques described in this book. However, much less is known about them for a number of reasons. For example, many of the activities viewed as normal hygiene care of infants (usually done by women) may mask potential sex offending. Furthermore, some researchers, in applying double standards, insist women never offend on their own, but rather in collaboration with a male conspirator. This is not always the case (Salter, 2003). Women do sexually molest both male and female children, and the harm they cause is as insidious as the damage caused by their male counterparts. However, because the information obtained for this book was based on data collected from thousands of interviews with male child molesters, the stories provided here will be based on information obtained from men. Current evidence would suggest some female child molesters behave similarly, although their actions may be more vindictive and cruel. Certainly, any female whose conduct parallels behavioral profiles described in this book should be considered as suspect as any male.

The molesters described in this book all use the same grooming strategies to ingratiate themselves with families and communities to obtain unimpeded access to children. Their strategies are such clichés, it would seem they had all graduated from the same crime school, where they learned how to successfully sexually abuse children with the blessing and support of the very adults and organizations responsible for protecting children. This profile was also observed in the publicity regarding the failure of the Catholic Church to protect children from abusive priests while continuing to support those priests whose conduct should never have been tolerated. The Catholic Church, however, does not have a monopoly on mishandling these cases. Information from hundreds of cases of identified child molesters from all professions, walks of life, and economic backgrounds reveal the same dynamics exemplified in the Catholic Church controversy, reflecting techniques already outlined elsewhere (van Dam, 2001) that exactly describe the operating strategies abusers use to successfully get away with sexually molesting children. Events noted in the Catholic Church only parallel how these challenges are often also mishandled everywhere.

Even after these Groomers are officially charged and convicted of a sexual offense, much of their predatory behavior remains invisible to the untrained eye. Many of these offenders continue to engage in their addictive habits, only becoming more sophisticated at evading detection. However, because their strategies are usually so predictable, and because like any addict they are continuously and actively working on gaining access to children to satisfy their addictive urges, they are typically much more recognizable than was previously thought. For instance, observing a liquor store when it first opens in the morning will reveal a swarm of alcoholics descending on it. In other words, knowing where to look and knowing what to look for can identify addicts because of their very predictable, goal-driven behavior. In fact, the addictive nature of the behavior makes them visible. Becoming familiar with a number of representative child molesters will begin to unmask the Groomer's profile.

The following cases exemplify successful child molesters. Their stories are based on thousands of in-depth interviews with child molesters. Should the individuals in any of these cases appear familiar, it is precisely because those type of child molesters are so alike in how they talk, target adults, and groom children. If any of these cases remind the reader of someone they know, it would suggest the need to take a much closer look at the known individual, and to utilize the scrutiny and caution recommended in this and other books to ensure the safety of children. Should this become frightening, it is because it is extremely difficult and dangerous to manage this terrain effectively. However, only accurate knowledge and understanding, together with close community support, can provide people with the power to eradicate child sexual abuse.

The descriptions in this book and all the words attributed to these child molesters, their families, and community members impacted by them are real, but these cases are composites of thousands of similar cases. Everything cited here was repeated in hundreds of similar cases. Though it may seem too astounding to be possible, the Groomer behavior in each of these cases is commonplace. These cases are not fictional. Similar events occur in every community.

Many people who are not child molesters are charming, helpful, and delightful, revealing only one aspect of behaviors also used by the Groomers. Such individuals, however, are not sexual addicts and their behaviors rarely are cause for alarm or concern to the people who know and love them. Rather, the child molesters who masquerade as caring and helpful individuals leave a wake of concerns behind them because of inappropriate conduct and innuendoes about sexual improprieties or boundary violations. In fact, this very difference will be more thoroughly addressed later in the book because of the relevance of such information in differentiating those who are innocent from those whose conduct is suspect.

THE SOCIAL PSYCHOPATH

Meeting Businessman Bob will help the reader better understand child molesters. This case is a composite of many similar cases that were closely studied. If anything about Bob's story seems familiar, it is because so many of the events noted among this population follow similar patterns, making this case representative of the observations made by so many individuals who have been impacted by similar child molesters.

Bold Businessman Bob

Bob is a successful businessman who is well liked in the community. His excellent social skills have resulted in others accepting him and tolerating his idiosyncrasies. He married Wanda, who for years wondered how she had become so lucky to have a husband as successful and handsome as Bob. While Bob was college educated, Wanda never graduated from high school. Bob had traveled and was sophisticated; Wanda had worked at minimum wages, and never left home.

They met at the restaurant where Wanda was a waitress and they married within the year. He set her up in an elegant home, after which she immediately became pregnant. They eventually had four beautiful daughters. Bob began molesting the oldest daughter when the girl was ten years old, although she only finally disclosed the abuse to her mother when she was fourteen years old. When Wanda heard her daughter's disclosure she was distraught, but despite the fact that she had few work skills and by leaving Bob she and her daughters would become destitute, leave him she did.

Bob denied most of the allegations, insisted his daughter had been the sexual aggressor, blamed Wanda for having gained weight, but acknowledged enough culpability that he was convicted. Because he had no prior criminal record and because he acknowledged some guilt, he was recommended for treatment through the Special Sex Offender Sentencing Alternative (SSOSA), an opportunity made available to eligible child molesters in lieu of receiving a prison sentence.

Once in treatment, Bob made an excellent impression on the therapist, and subsequently finished a two-year program with an endorsement that he was successfully "recovered." Most treatment providers would be more cautious in their recommendations, but Bob was very socially skilled, and benefited from having obtained a young and naïve treatment provider.

Within a few years, shortly after he was no longer under community supervision, Bob married a second time to a woman who already had two young daughters. He once again established himself in the community as the well-liked successful businessman that he was. He tried to regain contact with his own daughters, which Wanda did not support despite the fact that he had successfully completed all legal treatment and supervision requirements, and there were no longer any further constraints against him. Since Wanda would not cooperate with providing him with opportunities to see his daughters, he met them at school, helped coach them at team sports, and took them out during school hours for elegant lunches and shopping sprees.

The more Businessman Bob contacted his daughters through such means, the more enraged Wanda became, but all of her efforts to curtail his encounters with the girls only made her look hysterical, while he serenely continued spending time with his daughters and their friends. Despite the court's ruling that he was to have no further contact with this eldest daughter whom he had abused, he attended her school performances and closely followed her various activities from a distance. The court had placed no restrictions regarding access to his other daughters. Though Wanda felt he was "stalking" them, those who knew him were sure he was simply trying to make up for his prior "error in judgment."

His new home became a haven for adolescent girls, as he also encouraged his stepdaughters to invite their friends to visit and kept the home stocked with food and entertainment to please the girls. Businessman Bob was "rehabilitated." He had completed sex offender treatment and was now actively involved in the community. He had created a new family who lived in a desirable neighborhood, while Wanda and her daughters were struggling in a cabin without electricity, central heat, or running water. Wanda's daughters wore second-hand clothes, ate beans and rice, but were clean, healthy, and safe.

Bob, however, felt his more financially secure lifestyle would suit them better than living in poverty with their mother, and petitioned the court for custody. After all, he was a successfully treated child molester who had a stable home with a good income. His efforts to sway the court met with increasing success, and with each step in that direction Wanda became more and more distraught. By the time the case came to court, what the judge and other involved professionals saw was a haggard, hysterical, impoverished mother who made wild accusations against her suave and debonair ex-husband. To spectators, it suggested she was motivated by revenge and acrimony rather than concern about her daughters' best interests.

To the official and/or untrained eye, prior to Bob's first conviction for sexually assaulting his oldest daughter, there had been nothing overtly visible to suggest he might be a child molester. He had only one identified sexual assault, and everything worked exactly as it is currently designed to function, namely the child reported the abuse, the case was tried in court, Bob received treatment, and everything was resolved. Focused, in-depth interviews with family, friends, and neighbors, however, suggested many earlier indicators that should have been taken into consideration when evaluating his potential ongoing risk to the community after his first conviction. Had that information been known and understood, it might have been a helpful earlier deterrent to Bob, spared his identified victim(s), and generated more appropriate release plans, clearly indicating a need for greater collaboration between earlier victims and the criminal justice system. Chapter 10 provides suggestions for how investigators, earlier victims, and families familiar with the Groomers can help make the information available to prevent recurring sexual misconduct.

Numerous oddities occurred during Bob's adolescence that should have alerted people of his diverging sexual proclivities. For instance, at age fifteen the neighbors noted he was peeping in windows, but it was laughed off as nothing more than a boyish prank. The following year there were rumors that he had taken sexual advantage of a young developmentally delayed girl, but the rumors were discredited as an attention-getting ploy by the girl because he was so handsome and successful, and the girl in question was viewed as plain and overweight. When questioned by his parents, Bob convincingly showed concern for the girl's "delusions" and believably denied having ever touched her.

Further rumors kept following him, but each was addressed in isolation, and none were sufficient to tarnish his reputation. While he was in college the women he dated were mostly single mothers. His parents disapproved of these relationships because the women were older and had children, worrying that such live-in relationships created poor role modeling for children. Otherwise, Bob was thoughtful and considerate to the children. A number of these relationships ended when the women became jealous of his attentions to their daughters. In fact, one woman actually accused him of inappropriately touching her daughter, but he convinced her she was overreacting because of her own abusive background, so nothing further came of this, and he terminated the relationship.

When Wanda met Bob she knew nothing about these prior incidents. She described being swept off her feet in a whirlwind romance, and noted that he was scrupulously attentive to her. She was disappointed that this attentiveness waned considerably after the marriage, but assumed that to be normal. She became more and more uncertain of herself during the relationship as he would disagree with her perceptions, argue about the accuracy of her recollection of events, and refute minor points while belittling her about everything, all done with such subtlety, ingenuity, and finesse that she always assumed she was at fault. Long before her oldest daughter disclosed the abuse she began to become increasingly uncomfortable with Bob's attentions toward the girl.

Wanda had taught the girls about safety issues, and tried very hard to give them the confidence to be assertive. When her oldest daughter was fourteen, the girl disclosed the sexual contact by her father, explaining to her mother that the abuse began when she was ten, with the sexualized touching escalating in intensity and increasing in frequency over the years. She finally told her mother only when her father attempted vaginal intercourse.

Wanda responded to her daughter's information immediately by calling the police. Despite the emotional and financial difficulties, she divorced her husband and courageously remained supportive of her daughter throughout the subsequent ordeals that she presumed would culminate when the judge found her ex-husband guilty of having sexually assaulted his oldest daughter. She assumed this would ensure he would have no further contact with any of the girls, and that she could then proceed with the inordinately difficult task of independently raising four daughters with no economic support. She felt lucky to have obtained housing, and while conditions were grim, they were not harmful to the girls, who were learning how to grow vegetables, build fires, and haul water.

The system was unaware that Bob had, on many prior occasions, been privately accused of being inappropriately attentive to young girls. Nor did the system know about the numerous ways he was regaining contact with the daughter he victimized, contrary to court orders, or that he was again surrounding himself with adolescent girls. What the system saw was a very socially adroit and successful businessman who had been "cured" of his prior sexual proclivities. Tragically, the "system" did not appreciate the addictive nature of pedophilia, or understand the likelihood that pedophiles actively offend continuously. Since the system saw only the tip of the iceberg, Bob was considered a safe parent, an incest offender who had made one mistake, but had now "turned over a new leaf."

Therefore, unfortunately, the two identified interventions of the daughter reporting the abuse and Bob being convicted failed to suffice in revealing the gravity of the threat Bob posed. In the case that finally reached the legal system, everything worked as well as could be expected: Wanda had taught her daughters about bad touching, and eventually these lessons resulted in the oldest daughter disclosing the abuse, although unfortunately children often never tell. Then, Wanda credited her daughter's complaints, even though typically, children find that when they do disclose the abuse, their allegations are not believed. Miraculously, Wanda took the information directly to the police, who conducted an investigation that led to Bob's arrest and conviction. Most such cases are never similarly identified or adjudicated.

Bob was now a released child molester. He returned to live in the community, viewed as having paid the price for an "error in judgment." His petition to the courts to regain custody of his three younger daughters was granted. After all, he had a nice home, and a new wife who was aware of his prior mistake and who could run interference should there be any possible ongoing chance that he might misbehave toward any of the girls. As added security, the judge who granted custody to Bob recommended that future misconduct would be mitigated by having the girls put locks on their bedroom doors.

THE EAGER BEAVER

Some child molesters are particularly successful because they are so well liked and incredibly helpful that adults seem to wait in line to give them access to children. This profile is often seen, and in fact, the following story about Marvin is no different than the stories repeated by thousands of skilled child molesters. Therefore, should the reader recognize any resemblance between Marvin and someone they know and love, it would further demonstrate the need for becoming better educated on this topic to unmask those whose involvement with children should be suspect. Such marvelous men live in every community, and operate successfully everywhere. Marvin's story, with only minor variations in the details and the names, parallels cases unveiled in every town.

Marvelous Moving Marvin

Marvin was born in 1970, the oldest son in a family of five, with sisters two and four years younger. His middle-class family lived in a respectable suburb where his parents were well regarded. His father worked for the post office delivering mail on foot in the downtown business district, having worked the same route for twenty years, and knew all the customers by name. Marvin's mother ran an in-home day care when the children were young, then after the children were all in school she obtained a job as a teacher's aide at the nearby elementary school, a job she kept long after the children left home. His mother adored young children, supervised their activities on the playground, and remembered them long after they had grown up. In fact, some of these young charges came back to visit her every year.

Marvin had been an easy child to raise: He was cooperative, obedient, and quick to please. His mother never remembered experiencing the rebelliousness with him that so many of her friends endured with their sons during the teenage years. Even after he had graduated from the elementary school where his mother worked, he would often come back from middle school, and later high school, to visit her at work in the hour between his earlier release from school and the time the younger kids got out. In fact, because everyone at his mother's school knew him, he later sometimes even substituted for her on the playground for the last few moments while parents were picking up children so she could run home and get dinner started. Whenever he came to visit the playground the kids would clamor around him for his attention, run into his arms, and jump all around him yelling and squealing with delight. He would pick them up, hold them upside down, twirl them around, muss their hair, or join them in a tussle on the grass. His mother, and some of the teachers who remembered him, would bemusedly watch his friendly antics. Some of the mothers, who knew how much their children adored Marvin, would also ask him to babysit.

Marvin began babysitting by age twelve, and continued to do this throughout his high school years. As Marvin matured, the number of families who depended on him grew. As soon as he received his driver's license, the services he provided to these families only increased as he took their children to soccer, drove them to basketball, or chauffeured them to dance classes. Throughout his busy schedule he continued to get good grades, and never failed to meet his other obligations. The money he earned babysitting was invested in a van outfitted with the latest technology including a television, PlayStation, and even a computer terminal because he knew these onboard activities would make it easier to transport children.

Marvin's babysitting activities somewhat curtailed his social life, which his parents did not object to as they were scandalized by how his female peers dressed and acted. The parents were relieved to see how little interest Marvin appeared to have in these girls, but happy to note he was interested in girls as this reassured them he was not homosexual. He went to the senior homecoming dance with the beautiful daughter of one of their friends, where he behaved like a perfect gentleman. The pictures showed him with his blond curly hair, shy smile, and slim, tall build, standing with his arm around a pretty blonde girl in a blue evening gown.

The family was deeply religious, attending church every Sunday. They were thrilled to note that unlike so many of his friends, who rebelled against all the family values, Marvin accepted the teachings of the church. He was, in fact, extremely active in the camp program the church ran every summer, providing leadership and enthusiasm as a camp counselor years after he was too old to attend as a participant.

Both parents were very proud of him. After years of watching him be so responsible and easy to get along with, they trusted his judgment. They were able to get away for the occasional weekend, leaving him in charge of his two younger sisters, even while he was still in high school. Although his sisters complained whenever he was left in charge, the parents attributed this to normal sibling rivalry. When the younger sisters, who were becoming increasingly oppositional, objected to their brother's behavior, the parents discounted the girls' hateful comments as the girls refused to attend church, were doing poorly in school, dressed provocatively, and socialized with boys who had terrible manners.

Occasional problems arose. One boy Marvin babysat told his mother "I don't like Marvin. He makes me stay in the bathroom." His mother could never get any further clarification, but decided to not have Marvin babysit anymore. Another girl asked her mother, "Why is Marvin's pee pee so big?" Her mother did not know what to make of this question, could not elicit any further information from the girl, but worried. She and her husband decided to find another babysitter.

Marvin also began socializing with some of his young charges from church camp. The summer after high school graduation Marvin offered to take a twelve-year-old he met through camp on an overnight fishing trip. The parents found it curious that their child's camp counselor would choose to socialize with a much younger boy. The younger boy was flattered by the attention and eager to go on the expedition, but the parents said "no." Marvin continued to call their son with other offers, including outings to the lake, the movies, and a fair. The parents became increasingly concerned that an eighteen-year-old boy would want to socialize with someone so much younger.

Discussing this with friends and neighbors revealed a number of similar concerns from others: One boy had told his dad "Marvin crawled in my sleeping bag when we were at camp because he said his bag had gotten all wet." A little girl had been indignant because "I'm big enough to wash all by myself. I don't need him to scrub me in the bathtub." Two of the families who attended the same church as Marvin and his family overheard their children discussing Marvin: "I can't pee white stuff like he can. My pee is only yellow."

Through these discussions, the parents wondered whether they were making a big deal out of something best left alone. None of them felt their children had been particularly traumatized. In fact, one mother noted her son kept asking, "When can I see Marvin again?" Obviously, if Marvin had done anything to harm the children, the children would want to avoid Marvin. One mom, while watching the kids at a soccer game, happened to discuss her ambivalence with another mother at the game. That mother knew her neighbor's son had more specifically complained to his parents about Marvin, disclosing "Marvin touched me on the penis and he made me suck his penis."

Although this neighbor's boy was sixteen, he was developmentally disabled and both physically and emotionally much younger than his chronological age. The parents had taken their complaint to the police who told them there was nothing to investigate. These parents were told, "Your son is of age. It was a mutual thing."

Another mother at the church, who volunteered at the day care center, became increasingly concerned about how much time Marvin seemed to be spending in the bathrooms. Whenever she looked up he was accompanying yet another child to the bathroom. In all her years of working with children she had never noticed the need for that many bathroom trips. She happened to mention this to a friend who had overheard the conversation about Marvin on the soccer field. The mother who volunteered at the day care center knew these other moms and talked to them. Finally, feeling uncomfortable and embarrassed, she discussed her concerns with one of the church leaders, who reassured her that he would look into the matter. She never heard anything further, but it seemed to her that Marvin was now spending less time accompanying children to the bathroom at church.

One year later, a young boy told his parents that Marvin "put his penis in my butt." The parents went to the police, where the boy made this statement directly to the police. As a result, a police investigation was initiated. The police interviewed Marvin, who recounted:

> There were two police officers. They told me what this boy had said, and asked, "Is any of this true?" I told them, "I know that boy. I was looking after him when his parents were out of town." He had complained about an itching bottom, and I was worried that he might have had a rash or something, so I asked if I could check him out. I probably should have taken him to the doctor instead. I have no idea why he said that I put my "penis in his butt." I did use my fingers to spread his butt cheeks so I could get a good look to make sure there was nothing wrong. Then, so he would be more comfortable, I put some salve around his anus. I used my finger to do this. That's probably how he got confused.

The police were satisfied with their investigation and the matter was dropped. The complaining family was embarrassed about the event, felt uncomfortable about having gone to the police, and had difficulty returning to church because they did not know what they should say to Marvin or his family. Once again the matter was dropped and nothing further was done. Unbeknownst to any of the others who had complained about Marvin's behavior, a thirteen-year-old girl became pregnant, which forced the girl to disclose that Marvin was the father. The girl's parents were devastated. They had trusted Marvin. The two families had been inseparable, and Marvin had been like an older brother to this girl. They did not wish to report him to the police, and so they privately struck a deal with Marvin and his family: "Get counseling. Get help for your problem." As a result, Marvin went into therapy. Marvin reported:

> My counselor thought the whole thing had been blown way out of proportion. He told me, "You're only doing what comes naturally. Of course you're going to be aroused if you hang out with such sexy young girls." He recommended, "get a girlfriend," so I did.

Two months later, Marvin announced plans to marry. The parents whose daughter had become pregnant were relieved. Marvin's sexual misconduct would no longer be a problem. His fiancée, who was a few years older and recently widowed, already had two young children who both adored Marvin. Marvin instantly became a family man, and moved in with his new wife and children. He had never before been responsible for others, and took his new life very seriously. He opened up an after-school activity center that included something to interest every age group. For the younger children he provided games, activities, and birthday parties. For the slightly older children he offered overnight adventures. Since he was already well-known in the community, word about his new service spread and he quickly obtained many clients. Parents happily had Marvin arrange birthday parties, organize teen events, and provide outings. Marvin was delighted to be able to earn a living at what he most enjoyed. "I love being around kids. My life has always been kids, kids, kids. Now I get paid for it."

Marvin explained that about two years later,

> When I was about twenty-two, I started drinking more. As a result, my judgment was off. My wife and her kids were out of town visiting her mother. I invited some of the kids from work to spend the night. These were the older kids, and my intentions were to start training them to be staff assistants. Business was good, I was making lots of money. I was feeling pretty cocky.

The party at my house got a little wild. We made a lot of noise, and the neighbors called the cops. I was like, totally, not expecting this. So, when the doorbell rang I assumed it was another kid coming late, and one of the kids answered the door. She had a beer in her hand, and she was only fourteen. She got scared. The police arrested me for serving alcohol to minors. They interviewed the kids about the beer. One of the girls was undressed. When they asked me about it I said, "She was trying to put on her bathing suit and needed me to help her with the straps. If you don't believe me, go ask her." They accepted my explanation and never talked to the girl, which was lucky for me. By that time, she and I were having intercourse. If they had talked to her, she might have told them everything. I admitted to the police, "I guess I have a drinking problem. That's probably why my judgment was so poor. I should have let one of the other girls help her with the swim suit." I was charged with contributing to the delinquency of a minor, went into a drug and alcohol treatment program, and that was the end of it.

Marvin's wife was understandably upset to learn her husband had been charged, and worried about family finances during the inpatient phase of his drug and alcohol treatment program. Marvin returned from treatment more considerate and thoughtful than before, and the family resumed their prior lifestyle. Marvin, however, claimed that because of the treatment program, which included personal counseling, "I was a more together person. This meant I could do a better job of covering my tracks, keeping everyone happy, and carrying on." He admitted that by this time

I had been sexually involved with about 200 kids. However, I was finding that I wasn't that interested in the casual sex anymore. I was more interested in those kids I could have a relationship with. I had settled down. There were only a couple of young boys I was especially fond of, and there were three different girls I couldn't resist. What happened next was a mistake on my part. One of the girls I was in a long-term relationship with brought her friend over one night. This friend was something else. She was gorgeous, and fully developed. I got a little carried away. Usually I didn't do this without first having developed more of a relationship. But, after she was asleep I crawled into her sleeping bag and fondled her. She was sleeping in this little flimsy nightie. It was silky, and she was so smooth. I got this huge erection, and I figured she liked me, so I went a little farther than I should have. I had sex with her and she told her parents.

This girl immediately called her parents who picked her up in the middle of the night. They took her to the emergency room, where she was examined. The police were called. Marvin remembered

this time everything was different. They had evidence. I admitted what I had done and I was charged with one count of first-degree rape. Because there were always so many kids around, the police began questioning other girls. They had no idea that they should have been talking to the boys too. Anyway, I ended up with about five other charges. Like I said, since they had the evidence on the one rape. I admitted to that, but I got very self-righteous and said, "I won't admit to something I haven't done," and I denied all the other charges. They bought that. As a result, I was found guilty of one count of rape. Because I didn't have a criminal record, I qualified for SSOSA and didn't have to go to prison.

Marvin's wife divorced him. His business deteriorated as parents stopped sending children to his program. Marvin decided it was time to make a fresh start. His therapist was impressed with his progress in treatment. Marvin was insightful, always completed his homework assignments in a timely manner, and frequently confronted other group members who were less forthright about their sexual proclivities.

After completing treatment Marvin moved across the country. He was single, footloose, handsome, and extremely sociable. He was an excellent skier, and while looking for a new community, stopped at a ski resort. "I hadn't originally planned to stay, but they happened to be looking for a ski instructor. I got the job and the next thing I know is I've got a bunch of beginners trying to learn how to ski." His classes included students of all ages who would spend all day on the slope and in the evening would relax in the large heated outdoor sauna and swimming pool. Within a short period of time Marvin found himself spending as many hours in the swimming pool as he did on the ski slope. He was surrounded by half-naked boys and girls. "I thought I had died and gone to heaven. The kids loved me, the staff adored me. I had a place to sleep, free food, free skiing, and all the kids I wanted." Marvin worked there through the ski season, and returned for a number of years. None of the children he molested ever disclosed that the abuse had occurred while on vacation at the ski lodge. If the parents were ever later informed about anything, Marvin never knew.

During summer when the slopes were closed Marvin traveled. He still owned the van, which provided him with sleeping accommodations, and he toured the country, occasionally picking up attractive hitchhikers, going to bars, attending beach parties, and generally socializing only with older teenagers. "What I really wanted, though, was a more meaningful relationship. I was interested mostly in ten- to fourteen-year-olds by that time."

Marvin found a job as a school janitor in a small town. Through the job he met a mother who had been recently divorced and was raising three children on her own.

> I didn't really like their mom that much, but these kids were something else. They loved me. Their mom could see how nice I was to her kids, so getting together with her was easy. We lived together for about five years.

Marvin found the relationships he had with all three children to be emotionally and sexually satisfying at first. But after a number of years, "the kids were getting too old, and their mom was getting more and more demanding. She wanted to get married. I didn't like her and so I split."

Marvin admitted,

> what I found was that if I didn't stay anywhere too long, people just didn't put it together. If some of the kids started talking, or if some of the parents started getting suspicious, they didn't bother with anything if I left. So I started moving about every five years.

He molested fewer children than he had in his youth. "I wasn't as interested in the casual sex. I got to know them better, and they got to know me." In addition to having fewer victims with greater security built in, "because of the therapy I had to take, I knew how to cover my tracks better." Twenty years later he has remained a free man.

THE SAINT

Other child molesters manage impeccable home lives and careers to help mask their extracurricular sexual activities. Once again, it should be noted that Dr. Dan is a composite case that describes habits seen among hundreds of similar child molesters. Therefore, if anything about this case sounds familiar, it should serve as a reminder to the reader to take a closer look.

Divine Dr. Dan

Dr. Dan was a forty-year-old married man who had one daughter. He met his wife, Mary, during his first year of college. Both of them were shy. She had been brought up in a very sheltered environment, and had never dated before. He was thoughtful and attentive, and her parents approved of the match because he seemed to be a serious student who was getting good grades at school and had career ambitions that they admired. After they were married she dropped out of school and worked as a secretary to help support him while he attended school. Though she hoped to raise a family, he recommended that they put off having children until he was steadily employed and could support them. As a result, she continued to work while he first completed his undergraduate degree, and then finished medical school.

He had decided to become a general practitioner, and had wanted to work in a small town, which he thought would be a safer place to raise a family. He had numerous job offers, and the couple settled in a small town where he became the only doctor. He delivered babies, cured colds, and even made house calls. Everyone in town adored him, and he quickly became well-known, highly regarded, and firmly established.

Mary had one baby, a girl, whom he worshipped. Because he was making a good income, Mary was able to stay home and be a full-time mother, a role that she loved. However, as the years went by, it appeared that she was unable to have more children. Dr. Dan had hoped for sons as well, as he had wanted to take them fishing, coach their sports, and generally pass on the skills he believed only a father can give to a son. Since it appeared that he would never have any sons, he became increasingly involved in community functions where he could help out boys who did not have fathers or whose fathers were less available. He became a baseball coach for a group of nine-year-old boys. He was a "big brother" to a number of other young boys. He helped organize an after-school program for young boys who he felt would otherwise have nowhere to go. The town responded to his efforts by donating an old building, which was renovated into a meeting space for the boys. During the summer he took the boys camping and fishing. In the winter he took them cross-country skiing.

Mary was the main caregiver for her daughter during the first five years. She enjoyed being a mother, and found many activities to keep herself occupied. She learned how to sew, making clothes for her daughter as well as outfits for the dolls her daughter had collected. She gardened, cooked, baked, and canned. When her daughter started school she helped in the classroom. As the years went by, however, her daughter needed less of her attention and time, and she became increasingly frustrated at how frequently her husband was gone. Between his medical practice and his numerous community activities he was rarely available to the family. She knew that his work was important, and she enjoyed the financial comfort his income provided. There were times, however, when she wondered why he was interested in spending so much time with young boys, and regretted that he had been unwilling to focus that energy on coaching his daughter or taking her fishing, camping, or even cross-country skiing.

Over the years, occasional nasty rumors were heard. Once in a while a youngster would refuse to go camping, or wanted to quit the team. A few boys told their parents how the good doctor seemed to always subject them to medical examinations. One boy described how Dr. Dan frequently felt the need to take his temperature—always using a rectal thermometer. His parents found this to be strange, quietly supported their son's choice to quit the team, but did not say anything. Another boy felt awkward at Dr. Dan's desire to more closely examine his penis. When the parents questioned the doctor, he explained he was only investigating whether there was a need to recommend a circumcision for the boy. Dr. Dan was not the family doctor, and they wondered about his behavior. They too supported their son's desire to quit the team. None of these families knew of the others who had similarly experienced discomfort and confusion with the good doctor's behavior.

THE CURMUDGEON

Not all child molesters are loved and adored by everyone. Sometimes the people who live and work with them constantly make excuses for their gruff exterior and odd habits. As a result, those who know them often explain their conduct, minimize any oddities, and forgive them for their faults. This was true in the case of Coach Carl, a blue-collar man who had been briefly but unsuccessfully married. Throughout his long career he had made ongoing contributions to the community. Again, it should be remembered that Carl's conduct is a cliché and that his behavior parallels that of similar child molesters living in every community. Thus, if readers recognize someone they know when reading about Coach Carl, it would indicate the need to more closely examine the individual they know.

Cranky Coach Carl

Carl adored soccer. He had played semiprofessionally as a young man and had always been disappointed that his skills as a soccer player had not resulted in a professional career. However, he never lost his passion for the sport and his dedication to furthering the opportunities for other young boys from disadvantaged homes.

Carl had been born on the wrong side of the tracks. He grew up in a poor, working-class family, with parents who were heavy drinkers and somewhat verbally abusive. They were also physically abusive; Carl frequently had his behavior corrected with the belt. He took his punishment stoically, and put his energies into school and sports. In fact, sports saved him. He was fast on his feet, training he believed came from avoiding drunken parents bent on physical violence toward him. Because he was somewhat short in stature and slight of build, he never felt he could succeed in basketball or football. Luckily, they offered soccer in his neighborhood, a sport ideally suited to his body build and his ability to run fast.

After graduating from high school he enlisted in the army, as this would ensure his escape from home. The army trained him to be a skilled mechanic, making him highly employable. He was briefly married, but his wife would not put up with his temper, his frequent unexplained trips from home, and his drinking. Although he had wanted to have children and raise a family, after his divorce he put his energy into sports and began coaching boys' soccer. He told everyone that he knew the game and was an expert. A league was organized, consisting of parents who knew little about the sport but were happy to see their children engaged in after-school activities. Carl became the resident expert. The league began with one team, and within a five-year period added teams for every age group.

Over the years parents complained: Carl was gruff. His manner was offensive. He yelled at the players, and belittled children and parents alike. He brazenly pulled on children's ears, slapped their bottoms, told them they were useless, and on occasion would grab at clothing to pull it off. Sometimes the shirt tore off, sometimes the pants. Parents would usually watch in amazement, but never knew what to do or say. Children who talked back were benched or cut from the team. Parents who complained also found their children benched or kicked off the team. As a result, children begged their parents to say nothing.

League organizers became apologists for Coach Carl. When parents complained, the organizers would say, "That's just his style. He's an old-fashioned coach. He doesn't mean anything by it." Carl was the league and the league depended on Carl. No one particularly liked him, but everyone accepted him, worked around his idiosyncrasies, and made apologies for him. New families who expressed amazement or concern were quickly coerced into accepting this coach whose methods, while highly suspect, led to teams who won soccer.

Over the years Carl never remarried. He became close friends with some of the parents of the different teams he coached. These families would tolerate him, invite him into their homes, but never felt comfortable around him. They always found his gruff manner somewhat off-putting. However, they were also available to help him during the frequent trips that he was required to make. Thus, they would take over the coaching for a few weeks here or there, or they would water his plants and collect his mail. They knew not to ask any questions about where he went or what he did, because he would answer such questions with aggression. "It's none of your business," or "It's personal." Other times he would sarcastically remind them, "I do have a life other than soccer, you know." He would make them feel guilty for asking, and embarrass them that they would begrudge him some time away from the enormous sacrifices he made so that their children could enjoy and learn from a master like him.

CRUDE GROOMERS

Not all grooming child molesters are sophisticated, highly educated, or well regarded in their communities. Groomers operate at all levels of society, using many of the same strategies already described to gain access and influence with victims at every social strata. Hundreds of the offenders interviewed had histories of chemical dependency, relied on public assistance, and/or had frequently been incarcerated for various crimes. Many had histories of domestic violence, backgrounds of frequent fights, numerous traffic citations and regular driving violations, but nevertheless found women who gave them access to children. The following case is a composite of hundreds of individuals who, despite their sordid histories, were equally successful in gaining access to children through the adults they charmed.

Bottom-Feeder Buddy

Nobody ever accused Buddy of being a genius. He never did very well at school, and finally dropped out in the tenth grade. After leaving school he briefly held a few jobs in the fast-food industry. However, he did not care for bosses, found the work hours too long, the pay insufficient, and did not like the customers. He enjoyed drinking, socializing with friends, the local street scene, and the taverns. There were different places to sleep every night, new people to meet every day, and always someone with access to drugs and alcohol or a way to easily steal it.

As a young man Buddy had never been very successful with the girls. He had asked a few girls out before, but the ones he liked clearly were not interested in him. He discovered, however, "whenever me and my buddies would be hanging out in the tavern, the older chicks would always be coming on to me. They dug me." He liked the attention, and discovered that after drinking enough beer, these women looked increasingly attractive to him.

Buddy easily picked up women who took him home. Sometimes when he sobered up in the morning he would be disgusted with himself. He remembered the first time he woke up in a strange house, and saw Rosie in the daylight, and said to himself, "I can't believe I gave her the time of day. She is one ugly fat bitch." However, he enjoyed having a nice warm bed, rather than sleeping under the stars, and liked the attention as well. "She was all sweet to me in the morning, telling me how much she loved me, bringing me coffee in bed. I thought she was pretty ugly, but it beat being homeless."

When Buddy met Rosie's thirteen-year-old daughter, everything changed. "This was one cute piece of ass running around the house in her nightclothes." Buddy quickly discovered a new lease on life. "I was like her new dad. As soon as her mom left for work, I got to know my new stepdaughter, if you know what I mean." Buddy lived with the family for weeks. "I thought I had died and gone to heaven. I learned all I had to do was tell Rosie a few lies and I had it made." Buddy stayed for a few weeks, spending days drinking beer and making desultory attempts at house repairs, "just so she'd like keeping me around." He did the dishes, told Rosie he loved her, and offered to drive Rosie's daughter to her different activities.

> Everything was going good until her nosy neighbor started talking. This neighbor come over one time when we was alone, me and the daughter, and she didn't like what she seen. She told the girl's mother. She told Rosie she saw us kissing and hugging.

Rosie wept and Buddy left in a huff of self-righteous indignation telling her, "If you're going to believe that neighbor over me, then you don't deserve me." He wondered whether Rosie and her daughter would file a police report, so he left town.

For the first few months after leaving Rosie's house, he worried that he would be arrested for child abuse. He remembered always looking over his shoulder, wondering when the police would find him. However, when nothing happened he decided she was too heartbroken about losing him, and ashamed about having been so gullible to ever report anything to the police. This made him suspect that the more vulnerable the women, the better his chances.

> I figured in any new town, all I gotta do is go to the tavern, find me a fat old broad, buy her a few drinks and tell her she is sexy. I find out if she's got kids, then off I go with her.

The women he targets are easily led by his little lies, desperate for love, attention, and companionship.

With practice, he has refined this routine, noticing that the women he targets become even more doting and blind when he does the dishes, does some of the cooking, and offers to help look after the children. Over the years Buddy has often been accused of sexually inappropriate behavior, usually leaving town before anything happens. He has been arrested a few times. A number of times the charges were reduced to simple assault, and he would spend a few months in jail.

I got one or two child molestation convictions I couldn't get away from. One time this kid told on me, and the court didn't let me get away with it, but I only got two years. It wasn't no big deal. Then I left that town.

Chapter 3

Current Practices

Community efforts to protect children from harm often fail because adults who run into child molesters rarely see sufficient blatant evidence to file charges. An adult encountering a child molester may witness odd behavior, observe boundary violations, feel offended by invasive mannerisms, or observe unnecessary aggression, but no one activity is seen as warranting a call to the police to report a crime. Instead, adults who witness these minor offenses typically feel confused, but talk themselves out of it, or assume they have witnessed an isolated instance or a meaningless event. This happens because most adults do not understand the underlying dynamics of how child molesters really operate, nor do they wish to assume the worst of others.

Naïve adults inadvertently collude with the offenders and talk themselves out of doing anything overt because the person they suspect is "above reproach," and what they witnessed or know was "nothing really". Marvelous Moving Marvin continued to be respected and admired by most of the people in his community, despite the fact that his behavioral habits paralleled those of most of the well-socialized, most studied child molesters. Businessman Bob's acknowledged misconduct with one daughter was discounted since he was so well liked, highly regarded, and viewed as a success story after having completed therapy. Dr. Dan's excessive medical enthusiasm was never fully addressed. Even Coach Carl, with his cranky disposition and his blatantly inappropriate behavior, was tolerated, with allies making excuses for him, while soccer players and parents were intimidated into silence. Bottom-feeder Buddy was often equally successful because the adults he charmed desperately wanted to believe him.

In fact, many of the very behavioral patterns and habits that should have been cause for alarm were viewed as strengths. Coach Carl's continued full-time coaching involvement was seen as evidencing his caring for children despite his gruff exterior. Marvelous Marvin's quick willingness to help look after children was admired, and whenever it looked too dangerous for him he moved to a new town where he could start afresh, a strategy Bottom-feeder Buddy used as well. Businessman Bob's desire to make a home for his other daughters was seen as a testament to his character, rather than a cause for concern. Dr. Dan's thoughtfulness toward so many underprivileged boys was admired.

Although many upstanding citizens exemplify concern for others and do good deeds, they do so without ever once creating the concerns about inappropriate conduct that accompanied Businessman Bob, Marvelous Marvin, Dr. Dan, Coach Carl, and even Bottom-feeder Buddy whereever they went. Because the information about how child molesters consistently operate was not well understood by people encountering these offenders, none of the clues were seen in the correct context, and usually nothing further was done. Instead, a few concerned adults chose to simply remove their children from the situation, or keep a closer eye on things.

Society currently uses two approaches to mitigate the danger of sexual abuse to children: (1) teaching children to protect themselves, and (2) taking clearly identifiable offenders to court.

These practices are necessary, but insufficient, and predictably counterproductive when applied to those offenders who are welcomed into the community. The onus of responsibility cannot be placed on children to protect themselves from child molesters. Most parents have no difficulty understanding this when applied to other safety issues such as using hot stoves, going door-to-door on Halloween night, wearing seat belts in cars, or using helmets when riding a bicycle. Expecting children to provide the primary defense against sexual abuse is even more untenable when the adults, mesmerized by the offender's charm, invite the miscreant into the home. Children abused by such individuals understand the double message; say "no" to child molesters, but "adore our trusted friend." Adults should acquaint themselves with the known profiles of molesters to more effectively teach children about safety issues. Adults also need to implement specific tactics to facilitate obtaining a conviction and/or to ensure the safety of children after convicted child molesters are returned to the community.

First, adults need to take direct responsibility for protecting children. This can best be managed in the following manner:

1. Learn how child molesters operate in order to screen out those people whose conduct too closely parallels the practices of child molesters.
2. Become familiar with the Groomer profile. This will help adults take direct responsibility.
3. Better understand how Groomers operate to increase the efficacy of any disclosures. Teaching children about good and bad touching, and teaching them to tell trusted adults when anyone touches them in the wrong way becomes more useful when adults also are able to hear such disclosures, and are willing to consider that well-liked, respected insiders can be guilty of sexually molesting children.
4. When disclosures occur, community alliances, in combination with reporting to the authorities, become essential. No one should ever tackle this terrain alone.
5. Taking offenders to court is necessary, but cannot reveal the hundreds of victims and thousands of offenses already committed by any identified child molester without networking, nor can it guarantee a conviction without proper groundwork. Nor does protecting children from sexual abuse end with the conviction.
6. Convicted child molesters eventually return to the community where they often resume their prior activities. Protecting children from convicted offenders requires new levels of cooperation between adults, community organizations, police, prosecuting attorneys, judges, prison officials, and forensic experts.

Businessman Bob's case exemplified current practices, and everything went exactly as it should when Wanda took Bob to court. Wanda had taught her daughters about good touch and bad touch. She had warned them that no one was to touch them sexually, and she had asked them to tell her if anyone should do this to them. What she did not know was that while she was educating her children about this, Bob was already sexually touching his oldest daughter. The girl learned from her mother that what her father was doing was wrong, but she was confused.

He said this wasn't the same. This was his way of showing how much he loved me. At first he told me he was kissing me in a special way to show me I was his special girl. He would buy me treats, and he let me do things that Mom would never let me do. I thought it was okay. After all, he was my dad. I figured that when Mom was telling me about not letting anyone touch me, she meant strangers and stuff. Then, he tickled me and said this was our little secret. I didn't like it, but he always acted so nice about it afterward. It got weird. Then he told me it was my fault because I walked around the house in skimpy pj's. He said if Mom ever found out it would destroy her. I didn't want to hurt my mom. Then he started telling me that if I let him do these things it would protect my sisters.

The daughter endured escalating abuse for four years before finally telling her mother. Thus, even though the results took longer than would be hoped, the lessons finally worked and eventually the girl disclosed the abuse. This is unusual. Many children still do not tell about the abuse even after they have experienced a curriculum directed at educating them and teaching them to tell about any possible abuse. They do not tell for a number of reasons, including being afraid, having been threatened, believing the abuse was their fault, or being sure the events they experience do not qualify as abuse.

As soon as Wanda learned about the abuse she did exactly what should be done; she called the police. In many cases the police are never even contacted. When Rosie learned that Bottom-feeder Buddy was molesting her daughter she never called the police because she was too humiliated and ashamed at how gullible she had been. Both she and her daughter were just happy to see him go, which had also already happened to Businessman Bob before on a number of occasions. One of Bob's earlier girlfriends accused him of molesting her daughter but never reported this to the police. Instead, he convinced her she was overreacting. Two other girlfriends simply terminated their relationships with him because they were uncomfortable with how he treated their daughters. An earlier allegation from a developmentally disabled girl had been discredited. In none of these prior cases had the police been notified. Wanda was the first person who followed through and took the information she had to the police. The police investigated the case by talking to both the daughter and to Bob, and because Bob admitted to some of the behavior, having done so to avoid closer scrutiny about other conduct, he was taken to court and convicted.

Sexual abuse does not occur in a vacuum, nor is every occurrence of sexual abuse reported or adjudicated. Rather, the opposite is true and most sexual assaults never come to the attention of the criminal justice system. This has always been true, as demonstrated in the cases described in this book, and has recently been vividly exemplified by the hundreds of sexual assaults committed by a few priests over many decades that never resulted in any legal repercussions (The Investigative Staff of *The Boston Globe,* 2002). Not all children tell. Often, their disclosures are not understood, or not believed, and sometimes their disclosures are discredited. Even when children do tell about inappropriate touching, and the adults hear and believe the disclosure, this information rarely leads to criminal charges or in any charges that result in a conviction (Bolen, 2001).

For instance, a number of the parents whose boys were uncomfortable about Dr. Dan allowed their sons to quit the team. In the case of Marvelous Moving Marvin, many children told their parents about behavior that appeared worrisome, and some parents responded by quietly removing their children from Marvin's care. In addition, a few parents did complain to the police. The number of official allegations made, however, failed to reflect the frequency of his behavior, and the eventual criminal allegations did not at all parallel what he had done. Businessman Bob's willingness to plead guilty to molesting his daughter ensured that nothing further would come to light and made it possible for him to continue to live in the community. As an added benefit, his good attitude and social sophistication allowed others to accept his prior one instance of misconduct as an "error in judgment" for which there were no further repercussions. In the cases described in this book, as in most of these types of cases, these two strategies alone, namely relying on children to tell, and convicting offenders, are insufficient.

TEACHING CHILDREN TO PROTECT THEMSELVES FROM BEING ABUSED

Teaching children to protect themselves is done by talking to children about good touch and bad touch, telling them to disclose if anyone touches them in the bad way, and teaching them to say "No" and tell an adult if they are abused (Committee for Children, 2001). Although this is an excellent component in a child safety plan, it is insufficient as the *only* approach because it fails to provide adults with the necessary tools to more directly intervene in protecting children. In fact, much of the research indicates that adults tend to unwittingly invite many of the child molesters into their homes, schools, and communities. These offenders expressly groom the adult community first in order to obtain access to children. Therefore, placing the onus of responsibility on children to protect themselves from being abused would appear especially ineffective (van Dam, 2001).

Adults can do much to take more direct responsibility for protecting children by learning how to identify those whose behavior should be considered worrisome, and then taking on the adult responsibility of personally saying "no" to any of the earlier overtures made by such individuals.

TAKING OFFENDERS TO COURT

A number of cases of suspected sexual abuse are reported to the authorities, which can lead to an investigation, although not all cases are investigated (Bolen, 2001). Even those cases that are investigated are not necessarily substantiated. Recent studies suggest approximately 34 percent of investigated cases have been substantiated (Bolen, 2001), although "the majority of substantiated cases of sexual abuse are not prosecuted" (Bolen, 2001, p. 166). A variety of studies suggest that often fewer than 20 percent of such cases resulted in a prosecution (Tjaden and Thoennes, 1992), and some studies suggest a slightly higher-than-20-percent rate (Fineklhor, 1983; Sauzier, 1989). Also, many of the offenders prosecuted in court plead guilty to a lesser crime. In fact, sometimes as a result of the plea bargaining, the final conviction does not even identify the attack as having been sexual in nature, but rather may be listed as an assault, suggesting only physical violence. It appears that

> only if the case is prosecuted does the offender have a better-than-average chance of conviction. Even then, however, most convicted offenders spend less than one year in jail. In the end, offenders may be convicted in only one or two of every 100 cases of suspected abuse. (Bolen, 2001, p. 167)

Convicted child molesters who have no prior significant criminal history may be considered eligible for SSOSA (Special Sex Offender Sentencing Alternative) in lieu of sentencing, as occurred to both Businessman Bob and Marvelous Marvin. Convicted offenders who cooperate with an accepted treatment program can then avoid a prison sentence altogether. Although some of the convicted offenders admit to the crime, whereby they become eligible for such treatment, others deny any culpability, claiming they were framed, that nothing ever happened, blaming the child as the provocateur, or insisting the relationship was consensual and therefore not immoral. These offenders are more likely to serve a prison sentence, but eventually, most of the child molesters convicted of committing a sexual offense are released back to the community. Information regarding subsequent recidivism rates varies significantly; it is especially impacted by the aforementioned difficulties, and further limited because definitions of recidivism tend to be viewed as synonymous with reconviction rates rather than reoffense rates (Doren, 2002), as more extensively discussed in Chapter 9.

Unfortunately, the two alternatives, telling children to say no and adjudicating some cases, fails to utilize the largely untapped rich qualitative information that follows the path of the child molester but is rarely officially identified. As a result, the various facts about improprieties known to community members who experience the child molester do not appear in any criminal history, and therefore remain invisible to the authorities.

By the time he was twenty-five years old, Marvelous Moving Marvin had already sexually molested hundreds of children, yet most of these assaults were never officially identified. Had investigators known who to interview and what to ask, more of his sexual misconduct would have been revealed. Many of Businessman Bob's earlier girlfriends worried about his sexual proclivities, but Wanda was blissfully unaware of this history when she married Businessman Bob, and so were the authorities who investigated the case when his daughter reported the abuse.

People familiar with Coach Carl's background remember earlier complaints as well as one or two investigations by the police due to some allegations that were made, but nothing ever led to any charges being filed or to any arrests. Furthermore, every year a new group of unsuspecting children and parents joined the team and were assigned Coach Carl. They had to experience the challenges that previous parents and children had already endured, with Coach Carl always benefiting from the regular turnover endemic to coaching a specific age group.

Even though Bottom-feeder Buddy much more frequently came to the attention of the police, his vagabond ways ensured that the authorities in each new location had little information about earlier allegations, arrests, and sometimes even convictions. He quickly learned that most of the information was only tracked on a statewide level, and therefore the authorities in other states would not have access to his criminal misconduct elsewhere. Furthermore, most of his crimes were viewed as misdemeanors. He said,"No one takes those seriously," and rarely did any of the girlfriends ever report the sexual abuse, both because of their embarrassment, as well as the belief in each case that he would never do anything like this to anyone else.

Much of this extensive activity remains invisible to the authorities and therefore never results in further legal repercussions. Even convicted child molesters, however, return to a community wherein they may have limited periods of supervision. Once back in the community they can continue to molest children. Many of these offenders often describe their lifestyles as being relatively unscathed by the single conviction. Some move to new towns, as did Marvelous Moving Marvin and Bottom-feeder Buddy. Others return to their communities, as did Businessman Bob. In each case they quickly gain the confidence of friends and neighbors. What is ignored is that many of these offenders have a more extensive history of sexual misconduct than was officially identified by the courts, behavior known or suspected only by those adults who had direct contact with the miscreant.

Most of this relevant information never results in any arrests or convictions because the adults feel there is insufficient information to press charges, or instead decide to keep their children away. This was why many players quit Coach Carl's team over the years, why a number of boys stopped going camping or skiing with Dr. Dan, and explained some of Businessman Bob's relationship problems with the various girlfriends he dated before marrying Wanda. Marvelous Moving Marvin discovered that whenever too many people became suspicious about his behavior he could leave town and thereby avoid further problems, as parents would be relieved he was gone. The cases of Father John Geoghan (The Investigative Staff of *The Boston Globe,* 2002) and Robert Noyes (van Dam, 2001), detailed in other publications, further exemplify this pattern. Many people may be suspicious but these suspicions never result in criminal charges nor are they included in any later investigations.

For society to more appropriately navigate this terrain, all instances of child sexual abuse need to become more readily tracked, more openly and easily discussed, and more frequently followed. Adults must learn how to identify those whose behavior is worrisome, and take direct responsibility for preventing such individuals from having easy access to children. The known instances of misconduct and the subtle cues that should sound the alarm—all need to be carefully tracked and monitored because of the significance of the overall pattern.

Protecting children from ever being sexually abused cannot be managed only by the police, courts, and prisons because they do not have access to most of the relevant information. This has been recognized in other areas of law where public knowledge is used to facilitate criminal investigations. The Federal Bureau of Investigation (FBI) has learned to ask the public to be its eyes and ears by calling in information. The Amber Alert System allows the public to help intercept in suspected rape/abduction cases.

Had this system worked more effectively at the time of the sniper attacks in the Washington, DC, area in 2002, many lives would have been spared. Evidence later revealed that the culprits had already generated many complaints to numerous law enforcement agencies long before the killing sprees because of their blatantly suspicious conduct. Television shows such as *America's Most Wanted* similarly mobilize the public's observations to locate miscreants that law enforcement personnel would never have found without such help. In Utah, a family relied on such public help to locate their kidnapped daughter, Elizabeth Smart. Smart was identified by a local citizen after the person saw a sketch of the suspected abductor on television and notified the police. Such community-based law enforcement efforts have been fabulously successful over the years. Harnessing that data does not encourage vigilante action, but rather provides a useful alliance between individuals and those charged with managing public safety.

Community participation remains rare when it comes to preventing child sexual abuse. Correctly understanding the dynamics of child sexual abuse and harnessing the information available about the most active child molesters requires improved collaboration between everyone involved.

Chapter 4

Not All Child Molesters
Are Alike

In science, the word "understanding" when used in "understanding behavior" means having the ability to correctly control and predict future events. Society does not yet understand child molesters, nor does the community accurately control their behavior or correctly predict danger, as evidenced by the mounting number of child sexual abuse cases. Often, the very terminology that is used can help to either better clarify or to obscure the problem. The label *sex offender* is a generic term used to refer to a number of populations whose behavior may or may not overlap, as it includes everyone whose sexual behavior toward others is aggressive, illegal, and/or inappropriate. Some individuals limit their sexual misconduct to specific populations, namely raping adult women, while others focus only on molesting teenage girls or sexually assaulting young boys. The problem is, however, that too many identified child molesters engage in a variety of sexually inappropriate conduct toward others. As a result, the current taxonomy for identifying sexual crimes may, in fact, be misleading because it tends to exclude too many victim categories whenever an offender is labeled.

The way child molesters are described may cloud understanding. Current practices suggest there are offenders who only sexually abuse family members, thereby implying no other children would be at risk around them. Such individuals are often referred to as incest offenders, incorrectly implying they would never harm children outside their immediate family. In some communities this has led people to suspect that while an individual's behavior may be worrisome, there is no problem because, as one mother at a community meeting said, "Everyone knows child molesters only molest their own children, so there is nothing to worry about because he isn't around his own children here."

This is inaccurate. Many child molesters tend to molest any available children, only sometimes specializing in certain age ranges or limiting themselves to one sex only. Although some male child molesters are primarily aroused by adolescent boys (homosexual pedophiles), not all child molesters who select boys as their primary target do so exclusively. Dr. Dan appeared to be primarily focused on sexual activities with the young boys. Although he had a normal sexual relationship with his wife, he reportedly never molested his daughter, but was continuously aroused by the young boys in his care. One psychologist who knew Dr. Dan incorrectly advised community members that Dr. Dan was perfectly trustworthy because "He has sex with his wife. People who have sex with adult women are never interested in little boys." Coach Carl, who had been married once, similarly appeared to focus primarily on boys. He never coached girls' soccer.

On the other hand, Businessman Bob, based on conviction data, would look like he was only an incest offender, as he was convicted for having sexually abused his own daughter. As already noted, however, a closer look at his history revealed sexual improprieties toward a number of females, including peeping at neighborhood girls, raping a girl at school, serially dating a number of women for the purpose of having sexual access to their daughters, and sexualizing his children's friends. Many other child molesters are more like Marvelous Moving Marvin, and when fully cooperative with the authorities acknowledge experiencing sexual arousal to boys and girls, as well as adults (Silva, 1990).

Referring to some offenders as *incest offenders* may therefore be misleading. Some child molesters prefer molesting within the home simply because it is easier, they have greater control over the opportunities, or they feel more able to manage security. Such offenders often develop serial relationships, typically with partners who already have children in the age range they desire. They also often encourage these children to invite friends over, thereby creating additional opportunities to molest. This was exactly what Businessman Bob did. Marvelous Moving Marvin also chose women who had children, and after his first conviction changed towns and relationships every five years, but Marvin was sexually aroused to both male and female children, and sometimes also enjoyed having sex with adult women.

Possibly, rather than referring to homosexual pedophiles, incest offenders, or opportunistic versus predatory offenders, terminology cur-

rently used to describe these populations, a more useful generic classi-
fication system would be to categorize them as those who access
victims only after having first ingratiated themselves with the community and/or family, versus those who assault unknown victims, in other
words, "Groomers" versus "Grabbers." The reason for such a distinction is that the behavioral habits and patterns of the two groups are dis-
tinctively different, thus calling for different prevention and intervention strategies. In fact, knowing the modus operandi of any identified
child molester is crucial to preventing child sexual abuse, understanding the potential risk, and developing future intervention strategies.

GROOMERS

Most of the child molesters described in this book are "Groomers"
who go to great lengths to first ingratiate themselves with the families
or communities whose children they target. Such individuals will predictably molest some of the children in their sphere. They only do so,
however, after becoming acquainted and established. In many ways
they are less dangerous than the offenders who assault strangers because they are predictable to those who know their operating methods. This is not to say they are not dangerous, but indicates their behavioral patterns provide clues for identifying them and managing
them before they access children.

When such an offender is released back into the community after
having served a prison sentence and/or completing sex offender treatment, their socialization efforts can help reveal the possible resumption of sexually illegal conduct. For instance, Businessman Bob
would be expected to sexualize any girls around him, and good intervention strategies would have focused on his resumption of behaviors
that should be viewed as alarming. He was married again to a woman
with young daughters, suggesting that these girls would predictably
be at high risk. He was resuming contact with his daughters, and successfully convincing the courts that he should have custody of the
three younger girls. He was also defying court orders by going to his
oldest daughter's school functions under the guise of being a caring
father, thereby actually demonstrating his brilliance at ingratiating
himself with the adult community. Businessman Bob's behavior, like
so many of the Groomers studied, is entirely predictable, making it

possible for communities to collaborate in more effective protection strategies precisely because the behaviors are all clearly geared toward the goal of feeding the addiction, namely sexual contact with minors.

Some of the offenders who belong in this category describe taking as long as six months before they feel safe to molest the children around them. Others are more efficient at becoming accepted in the family or community, and feel they can molest with impunity within days of getting acquainted. In fact, when caught, most of these molesters blamed their subsequent incarceration on having become impatient, or for initiating the sexual contact too suddenly, before having adequately laid the foundation of trust. Typically heard are such comments as: "I got so excited I started touching him before I normally would. That's why he told."

Marvelous Moving Marvin's only conviction occurred precisely because he initiated sexual contact with a victim he had not first adequately groomed. Similarly, Dr. Dan's close call with the police also occurred because he had not sufficiently prepared the targeted victim. Although these offenders are dangerous because they are so successful, they are also manageable because community awareness and collaboration could prevent them from having any authority over children.

GRABBERS

Some sex offenders are more chaotic and less predictable in their behavior. They sexually assault strangers, attacking them on the street or plucking them out of their homes. As a result, in many ways these individuals are much more dangerous. This is because even well-informed and educated individuals would be unable to recognize the potential danger they present. Typically, they are unknown to either the children or the families whose children they attack. They are also highly impulsive. This book does not address the management strategies for protecting children from this population. However, as already noted, this "stranger danger" represents only a very small percentage of child sexual assaults.

Furthermore, because these assaults involve strangers, the community already has better strategies in place for communicating when someone like this comes to town. Community members publicly share information and suggest protection strategies. Flyers are sent home to parents when schools learn about any attempted abductions. Descriptions of the alleged offender's vehicle and appearance are publicly aired and readily discussed. After such announcements, parents accompany children to school, ensure children are not left alone, and implement other safety standards to minimize risk.

Grabbers also grab the media headlines and the television sound bites, but the dramatic menace they present to children tends to obscure the importance of the more subtle, more insidious, and more successful Groomers who generate most of the injuries and whom are the subject of this book.

Chapter 5

Common Misperceptions

The problem with child sexual abuse is that much of what actually happens is explained away, minimized, blamed on the victim, viewed as an accidental occurrence caused by the alleged offender's stress, lack of access to a suitable partner, a poor marriage or unresponsive spouse, or the result of drug or alcohol abuse. The behavior may otherwise be accepted as a poorly executed loving gesture, or a misunderstood attempt at "sex education." Often the abusive behavior is explained as "looking after the child's hygiene," or attributed to "looking after a medical matter."

When child molesters are questioned regarding suspicious behavior, or when they are investigated as a result of allegations made, they provide a standard array of stories to explain what was reported, or to soothe concerns about any directly witnessed improprieties. Only by correctly recognizing these stories as the cover stories that they are, can adults avoid becoming bogged down in the slippery details to begin taking the necessary steps to prevent further damage. In other words, the caregivers need to know how to pierce these smoke screens in order to hone in on the actual misconduct. Then they can take the necessary steps to directly protect children.

Child molesters are intrepid liars. They lie because they can, and because those listening want to give them the benefit of the doubt. They lie to themselves, and because they believe their stories, they sound sincere. Furthermore, most people do not expect to be outrageously lied to, and therefore tend to believe the stories. Those who unwittingly encounter child molesters and are not accustomed to the lies are easily conned. Adults who are not already extremely clear about the boundaries of acceptable conduct become easy targets and are easily hoodwinked by child molesters. Those parents who unknowingly are being charmed by child molesters accept the stories because they are not attentive to the inconsistencies.

these lies to avoid the awkward and embarrassing task of expressing disbelief empowers the child molester. Accepting the inconsistencies enables the child molester. Tolerating blurred boundaries ensures the children will be yet more invasively abused. Being too happy to accept favors for nothing, thereby becoming indebted, may put children at risk. Being too quick to overlook warning bells ensures children will be targeted. People unfamiliar with the clichés of these Groomers, their lame rationalizations and their outright lies, will be easily seduced into believing "nobody this kind and sincere could be guilty of any impropriety."

This problem is exacerbated by any ignorance about the difference between innocent touching and the sinister touching that child molesters use during "horseplay" or other screening and grooming activities intended to access children with adult approval. For all of these reasons, it is important to clearly know what constitutes child sexual abuse, thoroughly understand the nature of the child molester, be familiar with their attempts at exoneration, and not be fooled by their explanations.

A number of sexual activities should be viewed as child sexual abuse. Attempts by older people to initiate sexual contact with younger people should be seen as sexual abuse. Most of the sexualized activity is rarely directly visible to adults protecting children. However, because these adults are the essential first line of defense in protecting children from child sexual abuse, it is essential for everyone to clearly understand what constitutes child sexual abuse and sexualized grooming behavior that should therefore not be tolerated. The following definition is provided to help create a clearer understanding.

DEFINITION OF CHILD SEXUAL ABUSE

This definition is not intended as a legal definition, but rather to provide adults with a framework for understanding the need to pay closer attention to know when to respond and what needs to be done. Child sexual abuse occurs when someone with advanced knowledge, age, or power engages a more naïve, vulnerable, or weaker person into a sexualized relationship without consent. Because children, by virtue of their age and immaturity, cannot give consent, any sexualized interactions with children are automatically abusive and should not be tolerated. The interactions can include direct sexualized contact, as well as more indirect noncontact events such as peeping, exhibitionism, and frottage, that should all be viewed as abusive as well. These interactions occur in a climate where secrecy is maintained because the more sophisticated child molester knows secrecy is necessary.

For example, two young children with equal power in the relationship who begin playing touching games, exploring each other's private areas, on the living room couch in plain view of family, are too young and too naïve to know to keep the activity secret, and their interactions would be viewed as normal sexual play. Should one of these children, however, have previously been sexually molested by an adult, and therefore know to close the door, the activity ceases to be innocent. Children who have been sexually abused have, by virtue of that advanced knowledge, been robbed of the opportunity to engage in normal sexual play with peers. Although too little is known about normal sexual development among humans, peer-sexualized play among young children (ages three to six) would appear to be expected. However, this would no longer be usual among older children. The following are the parameters for defining sexual abuse:

- *Power Difference:* One person is older, bigger, more powerful and/or more knowledgeable.
- *Sexualized Activity:* The activity is of a sexual nature. The older person requires the younger, more vulnerable child to view pornography together, engages in exhibitionism or peeping, fondles the child or requires to be touched, as well as any more overt sexual activity.
- *Secrecy:* The older or more powerful person knows the need to keep this activity secret. Maintaining secrecy can be either explicit or implicit, and can be accomplished with promises or threats.

Clarity regarding this definition is essential as suspected child molesters will readily challenge or defy the possible inappropriateness of anything witnessed. Since only very little of what actually occurs is ever witnessed, adults protecting children require great courage, clarity of purpose, and knowledge to ensure that they see clearly, listen closely and correctly, and respond appropriately.

People often fail to understand that the most successful child molesters are those who have already ingratiated themselves with family, friends, or the community. Considering the possibility that such seemingly loved and trusted friends or family members could have dishonorable motives is exceptionally difficult, which makes it even more challenging to maintain clarity and resolve about what might be truly happening when questionable behaviors arise and concerns exist.

Typically, problems occur in two different ways:

1. *Something was witnessed:* Directly witnessing something worrisome is rare. However, with 20/20 hindsight after someone is convicted of a sexual assault, most adults recall various events that they saw and found worrisome. These adults intuitively felt uncomfortable with that person's behavior toward a child, yet talked themselves out of it. Or, they discussed their concerns with the suspected individual who successfully quieted their fears and made them feel foolish.

   Marvelous Moving Marvin described frequently having this conversation with many of his friends. In fact, he knew by the way that they approached him that they wanted to have "the talk," and he noted with pride that each time this occurred "they talked themselves out of it." He recalled they would say to him, "Marvin, you're a really good friend . . ." He would listen and nod, remain friendly and engaged, then "after 'the talk' they would thank me, and that would be it. In most cases, after 'the talk' I would continue with their child, only we'd be more careful."

2. *A disclosure was made:* At other times, a child discloses something directly to an adult. When this happens, however, the child might initially reveal only very little of what really took place because of fear and/or embarrassment. In fact, many offenders boast that even during a police investigation children typically tell almost nothing about what happened. Marvelous Moving Marvin bragged that when the police did start questioning some of the children "they told less than one-tenth of one percent of what really happened."

   Thus, a voluntary disclosure by a child can be expected to minimize the assault while giving vague and incomplete information. Should the adults hearing such disclosures then confront the alleged perpetrators, they can expect to hear an explanation that would allow them to heave a big sigh of relief, thereby avoiding all further difficulties and challenges. These explanations from the child molesters are such clichés that they are described here in order to provide the community with a better understanding of what they can expect to be told. When hearing such explanations, rather than avoiding the difficulties and challenges inherent to suspecting a known and trusted friend, it would suggest the need for better networking, further investigation, careful collaboration, and action.

EXPLANATIONS

Following are the stories that child molesters use to successfully allow everyone to assume that "nothing really happened." Once an offender has convinced the parent or other suspicious adult that everything is fine, they will often continue to molest that child, in which case the child will have learned that disclosing the abuse is useless because nothing changed. In fact, child molesters become even more emboldened when they know they have control over the "reality" of the observers, while the adults become meeker by virtue of the fact that they were embarrassed to have even suspected the possibility of foul play. Explanations that suggest the accused was only trying to help the child further ensures that the tables are quickly turned, with the child molester often even being thanked for his thoughtful assistance or helpful interventions.

Worse still, the empowered offender, often with the help of powerful friends and allies, may even threaten the suspicious adult for starting "vicious rumors." Since so little is actually ever directly witnessed, and since so much of what is known and/or suspected is uncomfortable, these strategies used by child molesters work all too well in stopping the adults from doing anything further toward protecting children.

One group of parents who were worried about a teacher's conduct toward their children complained to the school principal. That complaint resulted in a number of attacks against them. The teacher's lawyer threatened to sue them for defamation of character; the teacher's union threatened them with lawsuits. Other teachers accused them of being on a witch hunt. One of these parents said, "Everywhere we turned we were made to feel like we had done something wrong."

A number of the more frequently heard explanations are provided here.

Misunderstanding

All too often, little visible signs that would indicate the possibility of inappropriate touching or contact are easily explained away:

- One child told her mother the teacher put his hand under her shirt. When the mother confronted the teacher, he said, "Oh, I'm sorry. I didn't mean to make her uncomfortable. There were a number of children in the classroom who have all had the measles and I was just checking to make sure she did not have them."
- A wife heard that her ex-husband had touched her daughter's labia. When she talked to him he explained, "She was complaining about being sore and I was just checking her to make sure nothing was wrong."

Conspiracy

Often the offender will explain that the accusations were part of a plan by a vindictive ex-wife in a custody dispute, or an angry former girlfriend hoping to obtain a financial advantage.

- "Her mother told her to say these things about me so she could keep the house. It's a complete lie. I should have known because she did the same thing to her last boyfriend."
- "Her parents never liked me. They told her to make up this story. I never even touched the baby like they claimed. I was just giving her an enema. There was nothing sexual about it, but she just believes everything her parents tell her and they didn't want nothing to do with me."

Peer Play

Often offenders are seen engaging in tickling and wrestling activities, or jumping into "puppy piles" with groups of kids. Sometimes these activities occur with much younger children, but often are seen with teenagers as well.

- One twenty-six-year-old coach was seen wrestling on the grass with one of his fifteen-year-old players. In the process, his hands frequently grazed her breasts and vaginal area, with many adults nearby able to witness the activities. Most of the adults were uncomfortable with the play, but when one parent finally said something, the coach responded, "We were just having some fun. I find that my girls play better when we have a good relationship and easy camaraderie."

This inappropriate touching in public sends an added message to the victim. When such groping is witnessed by the adults, and therefore tolerated by adults, it confers approval on the behavior. Children experiencing this admit, "I figured they knew what was going on. After all, they saw it and didn't do anything."

Poor Judgment

Many of the thousands of child molesters interviewed explained the assault as occurring because of a simple mistake that evidenced poor judgment rather than any sexual deviancy on their part. "I'm not really a child molester. I'm not like those other guys who are here [in prison]. I made a simple mistake and I'm paying for it." These cases refer to sexual assaults by men in their twenties, thirties, or forties, having sex with adolescent girls. Often they describe the relationship as having been consensual. This can be a gray area when the boy is seventeen and the girl is not yet sixteen, which is discussed in greater detail in Chapter 6.

- "We both wanted it." The only thing that made it illegal, however, was her age.
- "I thought she was older than that. She looked older."
- "She told me she was eighteen. Can I help it if she lied about her age?"
- "She was really well developed. She was a knockout. In fact, she initiated it, and she obviously wasn't a virgin. There wasn't anything wrong with what we did."
- "She was my girlfriend. I didn't do anything wrong, except her parents got upset about it when she got pregnant. That's the only reason they pressed charges."

Other times the explanations refer to mistakes made or using poor judgment, but insisting there had been no sexual intent. For instance, one young father explained to the judge that his penis had only been near his baby's vagina to help him change her diaper.

"I was trying to wipe her butt, and she was screaming. I used my penis to hold down the diaper so that I could have both my hands free to get the job done. That's all that happened."

Medical Matter

Many times the alleged offender convinces others that the behavior resulted because of the need to look after the health and safety of the child. Nothing is ever mentioned about relying on medical staff or taking the child to the doctor. If the alleged offender is a doctor, as was true in the case of Dr. Dan, numerous opportunities for providing gratis medical care occur.

- "He seemed to have a fever and I was worried about him. That's why I took his temperature. A rectal thermometer is the most accurate way to get a good reading."
- "I knew you wouldn't mind my taking a closer look at her. She said she had a tummy ache, and I wanted to make sure she was okay. I only touched her on the tummy, I never touched her below there like she claims."
- "I thought he had a possible bladder infection because he complained of burning during urination. I helped him to get a urine sample, which I took to the lab and paid to have it analyzed."
- Marvelous Moving Marvin successfully used this approach when explaining to police his reason for having touched the young boy's anus. "He had complained about an itching bottom, and I was worried that he might have a rash or something. . . . I did use my fingers to spread his butt cheeks so I could get a good look to make sure there was nothing wrong. Then, so he would be more comfortable, I put some salve around his anus."

Parenting

Some of the offenders described the activities that they engaged in with young girls as helpful attempts to parent that were misinterpreted by others.

- One single dad claimed he was just teaching his daughter how to use tampons. "She was having her first period, and she couldn't get the thing in. She asked me to help her. I was just showing her how to use it and getting her started."
- Another man, seen touching his daughter's breasts, insisted, "I realized she was starting to get developed and she would need to go shopping for a bra. I was checking to see what size she would need so that she would know what to buy. I was just helping out. There wasn't nothing wrong with what I did."

Personal Hygiene

In many cases the accused adults deny any wrongdoing, insist nothing happened, and say they were simply helping the child with personal hygiene. These include fathers who continue to help their six- to ten-year-old sons or daughters bathe, carefully scrubbing areas they do not believe such children could be capable of cleaning on their own.

- "I was helping her to bathe. Nothing happened."
- "We were taking a shower together. We often do this as it saves water. I was only scrubbing her back for her."

Accidents

When the allegations are more extensive, or the witnessed activity more extreme, the explanations become more ludicrous. Too often offenders refer to these events as accidents. One can accept spilling a glass of liquid as an accident, but it is much harder to visualize how one could accidentally misplace one's penis.

- "I don't know how it happened. I was just minding my own business and the next thing I know that little bitch put my penis in her vagina."
- "I didn't mean this to happen. My hand just slipped and my finger somehow got into her vagina."
- "It was just one of those things. I was just sitting down, and she came over to sit on my lap. I have no idea how my penis ended up out of my pants. It was a mistake."

Sleep

Many of the alleged assaults are "accidents" that occur while the perpetrator is asleep and would reportedly never have otherwise happened. Often heard are parents who describe a daughter in bed with them:

- "I was asleep and rolled over. I thought it was my wife in bed with me. I didn't realize it was my daughter until after it was too late."
- One molester claimed he was such a heavy sleeper he would never be able to know what happened in his sleep. "I'm not aware of what happens. If she said I touched her, I might have. But I don't know what happens when I'm asleep."
- Another offender told the courts he was innocent, stating he suffered from a sleep disorder called "sexsomnia" that causes "violent acts of sex in your sleep." He did not believe he should be held responsible for his "illness."

Alcohol and Drugs

A number of assaults are attributed as resulting from the individual having a drinking or drug problem. Despite the fact that many people with chemical dependency problems never sexually molest children, this explanation is often accepted. This allows the accused individual to graciously enter into chemical dependency treatment without ever having to address the sexual deviance. In fact, child molesters who have done this successfully often describe that the treatment "made me more together as a person. This helped me get away with it more."

- "I would never have done this if I hadn't been drunk. It was the alcohol."
- "I must have been in a total blackout. I don't remember anything. It must have happened because she said it did, but I don't remember it."
- "I'm really a good person. I would never do anything to harm anyone. It must have been the drugs. I admit I do have a problem with drugs. But I've got that under control now. I'll never touch any drugs again, ever. I learned my lesson."

Seduction

Many child molesters blame the sexual assaults on the child "perpetrator," which unfortunately is all too often accepted by others. Even some judges have agreed that these three-year-olds can be provocative, making an offender helpless in the face of such a seduction. Often heard are comments such as:

- "What could I do, she was coming on to me. She was built like a woman."
- "She was walking around the house in nothing but a diaper. I didn't do nothing. She threw herself at me, and she didn't object."
- "Her mother knew what was going on. She let her little slut walk around in see-through baby doll pajamas. I could see her little breasts developing and she would just strut around challenging me to give her some. It wasn't my fault."

Sex Education

Most child molesters think of themselves as extremely helpful, and are the last to view their misconduct as problematic. Often, they initiate sexual contact after having begun conversations about sex education, thereby luring curious children to ask questions. Many of these children also assume guilt for any subsequent interactions because they did not terminate the earlier conversations about sex.

- One man was so sure of his innocence he did not consider the need for a lawyer. In court he explained, "Your Honor, I didn't do anything wrong. I was helping these girls. They wanted to know what a condom was, so I showed them. I had to have an erection to put one on so that they could see how it worked."
- A father convinced his wife that their thirteen-year-old daughter needed to be taught about sex. "He told me he read this in a book. If he could teach her lovingly what to expect, then she wouldn't be scared. She'd know what to do, she would be prepared, and she wouldn't get any of those dangerous diseases going around."

Unresponsive Spouse

Many child molesters explain that the only reason they initiated a sexual relationship with a minor was because "my wife cut me off." Often, the culture accepts this explanation, and a literature exists to blame some offenses on cold, unresponsive wives who therefore force their husbands to seek solace and comfort elsewhere.

- "My wife had gotten fat. It was her fault that she looked like a cow. Meanwhile, she's got this daughter running around the house who is hot. What could I do? I'm just a normal red blooded man. What did she expect? She knew."
- "I needed sex and I didn't want to bring home no social disease. I respect my wife too much to go out and get a prostitute. There was this little cute bitch running around the house. She liked it too. She didn't object."

The Best Defense Is a Good Offense

One thing that almost all child molesters use to good effect is putting the other person on the defense. Friends, spouses, and relatives of child molesters frequently note that they had been uncomfortable with a number of things the person did, but that any time they voiced any objections, the resulting spat became too onerous.

- One mother noted, "He wore me down. I didn't like a lot of the things he did, but if I said anything there would be a battle that lasted for weeks."
- One woman complained to her husband when she learned he had been drinking with her fourteen-year-old sister. He yelled at her. "You are so paranoid. Just because you were abused when you were young you won't let anyone have any fun."

Chapter 6

Accurately Differentiating Danger

Although many successful child molesters are never identified, or a tiny percentage of their sexual misconduct ever comes to light, innocent people are also incorrectly charged with committing sexual crimes against children. Most convicted child molesters insist they were falsely accused. Their protestations mean that truly innocent persons accused and/or convicted in error sound no different when proclaiming their innocence. High-profile academics reporting on false memory research and various vociferous organizations believe a significant percentage of allegations to be false, a perspective child molesters happily exploit. Others, convicted of child sexual abuse because of engaging in consensual sex with a slightly younger partner, fall prey to arbitrary legal-age cutoffs. They too are labeled child rapists. It is vitally important to resolve these problems both to protect the innocent, to stop the guilty from causing further harm, and to "steal the thunder" from offender apologists who dramatically use isolated cases of the falsely accused to exonerate the guilty.

Suffice it to say that child sexual abuse does occur, and it occurs frequently (Bolen, 2001; The Investigative Staff of *The Boston Globe,* 2002). However, errors are made. Many of these mistakes could be corrected by better understanding how child molesters operate. This awareness would reveal that the behavior patterns of the falsely accused do not fit the profile of the typical child molester, making it less likely they committed such crimes. Also, some teenagers, by virtue of their age and activity, may incorrectly be grouped with child molesters. Other molesters, keenly aware of legal repercussions, carefully avoid prosecution by refraining from sexual contact with underage victims.

Differentiating the innocent from the guilty can be done because the Groomers described in this book are sexually addicted, and as a result they are continuously engaged in activities that provide access to children and opportunities to molest children. The addictive quality of the behavior often distinguishes those who are child molesters from the falsely accused. Although many Groomers are also sexually involved with adults, this should not be seen as negating or ameliorating their interest in children. In fact, a number of very active child molesters pride themselves on being aroused by a variety of stimuli, boast that they fantasize about children when engaged in sexual activities with adults, or admit they endure adult sex to protect their cover (Silva, 1990). This book focuses on the sexual addicts who are aroused by children. This book is not about sex addicts who only engage in sexual activities with consenting adults.

The Groomers described in this book are sexually aroused by children, and act on these urges. They groom families and communities to access children, and because they do so on a continuous basis, they behave differently than the innocent. This difference, while crucial, can be discovered, not by looking at the tip of the iceberg, but by correctly incorporating information only visible beneath the surface for those who know where to look.

At this time it is unknown how many innocent individuals are falsely accused of sexually molesting children. What is known, however, is that among the Groomers under discussion, innuendoes, concerns, allegations, and problems follow them almost continuously. In other words, they generate a trail of slime rarely visible when relying only on conviction data, but identifiable to those who know where to look. Such a trail of slime does not accompany the falsely accused precisely because they do not fit the Groomer profile, i.e., engaging in image management with adults to access children, busily pursuing children through various activities, and constantly violating boundaries with children and the adults responsible for children. The innocent do not generate dozens of rumors, numerous complaints, continuous controversies, frequent scandals, and often-witnessed improprieties.

For example, most parents watch dozens of coaches during the years that their children play sports. Both volunteer coaches and paid professionals help their children learn the rudiments of each sport. Almost never do complaints about coaching include suggestions of sexual improprieties. Parents might find coaches too strict or not strict enough. They might complain that their children are benched too often, or be disgruntled regarding the coach's lack of expertise about the sport. These are expected complaints. Rarely heard are worries about inappropriate touching. Yet over the years, many parents wondered about Coach Carl's conduct, always with specific fretting about sexual improprieties.

This trail of complaints, innuendoes, and concerns tends to follow most of the grooming child molesters whose misconduct finally leads to a charge and conviction, as happened to Marvelous Moving Marvin, and Businessman Bob. Even Dr. Dan and Coach Carl generated a trail of complaints, worries, and questions, despite the fact that their conduct had not resulted in legal repercussions.

The differences between the behavioral habits of the grooming child molesters and those who are not child molesters must be utilized to both protect the innocent and more correctly identify the guilty. A number of cases will be more closely examined to help the reader better understand these differences.

THE UNCHANGING NATURE
OF THE GROOMER'S PATHOLOGY

The following case is again a composite of events frequently seen among the guilty. People like Predictable Peter operate in every community.

Predictable Peter

Peter was seventy years old when he was first convicted for sexually assaulting one of his grandchildren. Until this conviction, he had been a very successful man, recently retired after having had a lucrative career. He had been married to the same woman, having celebrated their fiftieth wedding anniversary just before he was sentenced. They had four children who were all law-abiding citizens, happily married, raising families, and with good careers. Peter had no criminal history. He had never been arrested, and he was viewed as a fine, upstanding member of the community. Peter pled not guilty and when he was convicted for sexually assaulting his seven-year-old granddaughter the community was shocked.

On the surface, it would appear that this one instance had been an aberration or even a wrongful conviction. Peter continued to deny his guilt, though this cost him almost certain diversion into SSOSA with no jail time because he was a first offender. "I didn't do it. I don't

know why she made up those stories about me. I never touched her."
He repeated this to everyone who would listen, but because the granddaughter was so explicit and her parents were so supportive of the
girl, Peter ended up in prison.

Although Peter's official record was unblemished, those who knew
him had always been suspicious. When his daughters were little they
complained to their mother about Peter's roving hands. Their friends
all thought he was a "dirty old man," and whenever any girls were in
the house great efforts were made by everyone to avoid him. His wife
had fielded a number of complaints from neighbors and had even
agreed to stop being a Girl Scout den mother just to prevent giving her
husband more access to young girls. Over the years his wife thought
she had protected her daughters by making sure that they were never
left alone with their father.

When the granddaughter reported the abuse, Peter's own daughters
confirmed that they too had been molested when they were younger.
Only then did Peter's wife learn her efforts to protect the girls from sexual abuse had failed. Peter's much-observed groping and grabbing had
only been the tip of the iceberg. He had repeatedly raped all four of his
daughters. They had never before told one another or their mother (assuming they were the only one), thinking that by tolerating the rapes they
were protecting the others from harm. When the granddaughter told, she
opened up Pandora's box. The sisters began talking to one another, and
the family members began learning the truth about Peter's life of crime.

In prison, Peter began suffering from Alzheimer's disease, remem-
bering less about himself and the world around him every day. When
Alzheimer's finally robbed him of all memory and any dignity, the remaining primal function of his personality was the sexual predation.
In the hospital where he was housed, each of the nurses responsible
for his care described how he would continuously try to grab them,
pinch a breast, squeeze a bottom, or clutch the vaginal area whenever
they had to step near him to bring him food, medication, or look after
his hygiene. In fact, when he was not actually grabbing and groping,
he was calling to them, trying to lure them to his bedside with candy.

Age and disease had robbed Peter of everything but his sex-offending, addictive urges and behavior, which were suddenly unmasked
and laid bare for all to witness. His continuous sex-offending acts in
the Alzheimer's hospital setting replicated everything he had done
whenever possible toward the young girls around him throughout his

life. Peter's one conviction occurred in the context of a lifetime of sexual addiction and assault. This sexual addiction remained long after all other vestiges of personality had left. Peter's story is typical of most of the cases under investigation, with the only meaningful exception being that in his case the sexually aberrant behavior he engaged in throughout his life suddenly became blatantly visible due to his brain disease.

A tidal wave of continued concerns about sexual improprieties and ongoing evidence of misconduct typically follows the well-socialized Groomer. This is consistent with information provided by thousands of child molesters. Offenders who divulge the truth about themselves admit to ongoing, full-time activities intended solely for gaining access to children for sexual purposes, e.g., "It was always in the back of my mind. Anytime I did anything, I was always aware that it would get me closer to her kids. That's why I was such a good guy." Other offenders admit that everything else they did "was only a smoke screen to let me get away with it." When Predictable Peter could no longer maintain that smoke screen, his continuous, sexually motivated, molesting behavior suddenly became blatantly visible.

Future research might help establish a natural break between those whose conduct never raises any concerns, those who have had the bad fortune to have been suspected once, or maybe even twice, and those who are constantly followed by complaints about their behavior. Although Predictable Peter might initially appear to have been falsely accused, subsequent evidence suggested otherwise. As in the case of Predictable Peter, many of the worries voiced over the years include neither conviction data nor charges and allegations, but rather reflected community information typically not tapped when conducting legal investigations. What became plainly visible in Predictable Peter's case due to his Alzheimer's disease, can be made more visible whenever a Groomer is investigated using qualitative data-gathering techniques.

This was further exemplified by developments in the Catholic Church. Cases such as Father Geoghan, and that of many of the other priests whose sex-offending conduct only belatedly received public attention, exemplified the continuous problems they engendered wherever they went. For each of those priests, their misconduct was often so blatant that it eventually came to the attention of the authorities, namely the church, in every community where they lived because of problems they created in every parish. Despite ongoing allegations in every new community where they were transferred, they continued to be reassigned to new communities, and because they were sexual addicts, they continued to sexually molest children.

In other cases, employers may not have been as directly aware of the sexual improprieties as was true in the Catholic Church because other organizations do not have such international hierarchies. One school district may never have learned about improprieties in another district or state. When hiring a teacher, schools do not have access to international records available to Catholic Church officials. Educator Robert Noyes was a prolifically active child molester whose misconduct became known by every school district in which he worked. Every transfer to another district included only glowing recommendations about his competencies and accomplishments, leaving each new district unaware of information already known by other districts.

In case after case involving these Groomers, however, complaints do eventually arise. In fact, in every closely studied case of a child molester busily "working" a community, responsible groups have ignored complaints and made excuses for these offenders again and again. It is no accident that the Groomer is so popular with colleagues and clients that they rush to his defense. That is the goal of image management, which Groomers do to facilitate access to intended victims. Their skillful efforts often result in a variety of public accolades, including awards such as "Man of the Year," "Volunteer of the Year," and "Teacher of the Year," expressions of community gratitude for their good works. Not all citizens receiving such accolades are child molesters. Rather, child molesters, because of their efforts at image management, often seek such public recognition.

Despite the image management, complaints do occur, but are frequently ignored, hushed up, or discounted. The soccer league was so used to hearing complaints about Coach Carl that they anticipated these complaints, referring to his coaching style as "old-fashioned" and therefore likely to be offensive to parents. This did not mean the soccer league condoned Carl's conduct, but rather that they were co-opted.

FALSE ALLEGATIONS

Unfortunately, innocent people can be accused of sexual misconduct and find their lives destroyed. The problems caused by false accusations typically reflect ignorance about grooming behavior and improper investigations. The following case is also a composite case that addresses the problems created for those falsely accused, further suggesting the need for a thorough understanding of child sexual abuse and investigation protocols to protect the innocent.

Truthful Tim

Like Peter, Tim had never been accused of sexual misconduct. He had been a high school teacher for almost twenty years before returning to graduate school to become a school counselor. For the next ten years he worked with troubled teenagers through the school. He was well liked and highly regarded.

Tim married, raised a family, and enjoyed close, enduring friendships with adults. When Tim was fifty-five years old a younger female colleague at school began flirting with him, making him increasingly uncomfortable with her preposterous behavior. At staff parties she would become drunk and throw herself at him. Tim did not care for her when she was sober, and liked her less when she was drunk, and increasingly avoided her, something that was hard to do since they worked together in the same school. In fact, she was offended when he spurned her, and in a drunken rage one night she accused him of having sexually abused her ten years earlier when she was a high school student where he taught.

The accusation was made loudly and publicly at a party. All his colleagues were there. Another staff counselor took the woman aside and began talking to her more closely to better understand what had happened. Tim was mortified. No one said anything to him, but the silence was deafening. He felt that protesting his innocence would further credit her story. For months he continued to work in the same school with this woman, something he found intolerable. Throughout that time an internal investigation was conducted, and it was finally determined that this woman had not even been a student at the high school where Tim had been teaching at that time, thereby making her accusation impossible. She dropped her charges, and nothing further was done except that for Tim, the allegations had forever changed the political climate at work. Shortly thereafter he felt the need to resign.

A closer look at Tim's life suggested none of the history usually seen among those who do sexually molest. He had solid friendships with adults, and was a supportive friend without engaging in the image management so often seen among offenders. He certainly associated with children the ages of his children, but only because he had children. He did not go out of his way to make contact with children, nor did he continue to seek out children in specific age ranges. He empowered his children, supported them in their activities, and encouraged their close friendships with others. Sex offenders, who worry that their victims might "reveal" what is really happening, socially isolate their victims or keep them too busy to let them get close to others in order to further ensure secrecy. His relationships with friends were a mutual collaboration of achieving shared goals, not the saintly helpfulness of someone too good to be true.

More important, throughout his long history in the same community no innuendoes of any sexual misconduct existed. No one had ever experienced anything suggestive of sexual improprieties in his behavior toward children. Tim, unlike Peter, or any of the other sex offenders described in this book, had none of the habits typically seen among sex offenders. Had staff been aware of the dynamics of child sexual abuse, understood the well-socialized Groomer sex offender phenomena, and provided a proper investigation by trained professionals rather than relying on an internal investigation, things would have quickly been put in the correct perspective. His accuser, correctly unmasked as having made false accusations, should have found it intolerable to continue working there, rather than Tim being the one to experience the discomfort.

Even while being investigated, his protestations of innocence were different from those given by child molesters. He did not vilify her, but rather described his frustrations at a system that failed to adequately understand and investigate the various dynamics. Throughout his ordeal he genuinely worried about the welfare of others.

GRAY AREAS IN TERMS
OF AGE AND CONSENT

Another area in which behavior may be incorrectly labeled as child sexual abuse would be in relationships between two adolescent peers engaged in consensual romantic activities. For instance, a fifteen-year-old high school sophomore female and her eighteen-year-old high school sophomore boyfriend who engage in sexual relations would not necessarily constitute child sexual abuse, unless rape occurred. However, if the girl's parents choose to press charges, the boy could incorrectly become tarred with the same brush used to label child molesters. Real child molesters, of course, use this argument in their defense when blurring the boundaries, claiming they were discriminated against on the basis of age. However, this argument becomes less credible as the age difference becomes increasingly greater, or in the context of individuals whose behavioral habits more closely mimic those of Groomers. The following composite case again is intended to help clarify this problem.

Innocent Isaac

Isaac was sixteen and a freshman at high school when he first began dating Sally, who was not quite fourteen, but also a freshman at the same school. Isaac was older than most of the other students in his grade because his birthday was in September, a week after the cut-off for starting school. He had also been held back an extra year when he first moved to America from his native country because he did not yet speak the language. By the time he repeated the second grade, however, he spoke fluent English.

Sally and Isaac were in some of the same classes. They would get together to do homework; they went to football games and other outings, and spent hours on the telephone. They had many friends in common, and enjoyed the same things. Both Sally and Isaac's parents expected this romance to go the way of all other adolescent romances, and assumed that the youngsters would quickly gravitate to other pursuits. However, Sally and Isaac remained true to each other, and swore a pact of loyalty. They became increasingly inseparable, and the hand holding, kissing, and hugging they had enjoyed for the first few months aroused strong feelings in both of them.

By the time Isaac turned seventeen, his beloved Sally was still only fourteen, and they had both become sophomores. The kissing, hugging, and fondling inevitably led to intercourse, although they had few opportunities to be private enough to have sex. They loved each other, went everywhere together, and held hands in public. Sally's parents liked Isaac, but worried at how much time the two spent together. Eventually, they began to intervene, but when they demanded that she stop seeing him altogether she revealed her love for him, at which point she admitted that she was no longer a virgin. Her parents were furious. By that time Sally was only fifteen, while Isaac had just turned eighteen. Despite Sally's anger, screams of anguish, and humiliation, they called the police and charged Isaac with committing a sexual assault against their daughter.

When interviewed by the police, Isaac admitted that he and Sally had sexual intercourse together, that he loved her, and that he hoped to marry her after they had both finished their education. Although his dreams might sound naïve, they were sincere, but because of his age in relationship to Sally's, he was charged as being a child molester. Since he had no prior legal history, he was offered the SSOSA program in lieu of a prison sentence. However, he was also told that he would be considered a child molester for the rest of his life and would always have to register as a child molester. It remained unclear whether he would ever be allowed to have access to children.

Isaac loved Sally, who was his contemporary, even though she was younger. Their relationship was truly a peer relationship. Both were high school students who shared the same friends. Isaac had none of the behavioral markers associated with child molesters: He did not seek contact with children, and had never engaged in the sexualized play usually seen among the child molester population. Although it may not have been wise for him to have sexual intercourse with someone younger, the relationship was truly consensual, with both participants having equal power. Sally was not coerced into sex with a more powerful partner, nor was she seduced by a more mature or sophisticated assailant. She made her own choices. Isaac did not babysit children the way Marvelous Marvin did. He did not force himself on Sally. They were peers in every sense.

The prisons are filled with child molesters who claim they were wrongly convicted for having sex with a consenting peer. In some cases this is true, and they are incorrectly called child molesters. Unfortunately, many *are* child molesters justifying their misconduct. Twenty-year-old men claiming emotional immaturity as the reason for becoming sexual with fourteen-year-old girls is very different from two school chums having a sexual relationship. Twenty-year-old men insisting, "She looked older," or moaning, "How was I to know she was only thirteen?" is not about peer relationships, but rather an opportunistic response to rationalize criminal conduct. A better understanding of the underlying dynamics of sexual abuse and greater clarity regarding the true histories of the individuals involved would correctly differentiate between peer romances and sexual offenses.

AGE CUTOFFS THAT DECRIMINALIZE
CHILD SEXUAL ABUSE

Although Truthful Tim and Innocent Isaac should never have been viewed as Groomers, other individuals carefully groom older children for sexual purposes but avoid detection because of their cunning awareness of the laws. Children over the age of sixteen are viewed differently than minors. A number of Groomers carefully refrain from any sexual contact until after the child's sixteenth birthday. As a result, they can avoid being labeled as child molesters despite the fact that their conduct exemplifies the Groomer profile and should be considered sexually abusive.

Judge Gary Little

Gary Little was a juvenile court judge in Seattle, Washington, during the 1960s. Between then and the early 1990s, when investigators were finally closing in on him and he committed suicide, he used his position of power to sexually molest hundreds of young boys. In the 1960s he telephoned boys after they appeared in his court to ask, "How are you doing?" Parents might have been happy that their sons benefited from such a responsible and caring judge. Boys who responded to these early advances were later seduced, but rumors circulating about Gary Little's sexual proclivities did little to prevent him from enjoying continued professional success. He served in several high positions in the Washington State Attorney General's Office, and then became a state supreme court judge.

Gary Little also worked at a prestigious private boys' school. But throughout his known thirty-year history of sexual misconduct, he escaped legal repercussions because he waited until the boys were sixteen, the legal age of consent, before initiating the sexual contact. As a result, his molesting was technically not criminal, but nevertheless predatory, cunning, exploitive, and goal-directed.

One of his young victims described how he was seduced:

> I was participating in a University Model Congress as a freshman and Gary Little was the advisor. I was interested in a political career and Gary took me under his wing telling me he thought I had a bright future. One time he took me to lunch with Governor Dan Evans and the attorney general. He arranged for me to do some of the

research for one of the governor's speeches. I was absolutely daz-
zled by his charm, intelligence, and high-powered political connections. One night at his place he said to me, "I'm going all the
way to the White House and I'm willing to take you with me if
you prove you are made of the right stuff. In order to pass the test,
you have to prove to me that you have the ruthless ambition every
successful politician must have. You have to be willing to do
whatever you have to do to get power. Have sex with me tonight
and I'll know that you have what it takes."

This student was twenty-five years younger than Gary Little, only
eighteen years old, with dreams of success and national prominence
that Gary Little cleverly exploited. After the sexual encounter, none
of the promises materialized, Gary Little became scarce, and this
young man remained forever haunted by shame and doubt about his
masculinity, and subsequently died prematurely. Legally he was a
consenting adult. In actuality, he was a victim of child sexual abuse.

Gary Little fit the Groomer profile perfectly, but was never charged.
His use of the arbitrary age cutoff was a brilliant strategy, allowing him to
spend years presiding on the bench of the state supreme court by day
while abusing boys by night. Detectives vainly tried to investigate the
case, but encountered victims too embarrassed to speak, and never
identified a victim under the age of sixteen. King TV News in Seattle
filmed an investigative documentary, interviewing victims with their
faces hidden. The night before the documentary was scheduled to air,
Gary Little committed suicide. This man's conduct should be viewed
as sexually abusive because he manipulated far younger, naïve, and
impressionable boys, abusing his power and prestige.

A GROOMER PROFILE: DIFFERENTIATING THOUGHTFUL FROM MANIPULATIVE

Although Gary Little's conduct should be viewed as fitting the
Groomer's profile, not all people who are helpful and caring are child
molesters. The following case is presented to help the reader understand that thoughtfulness and an interest in the development of younger individuals does not confer Groomer status. Rather, the Groomer
pretends to be thoughtful in order to gain access, a manipulative ploy
that is entirely self-serving.

Helpful Harry

Helpful Harry was above reproach. His colleagues called him a "saint" without any intended irony. He always worked longer hours to help colleagues who were behind. He never said an unkind word about anyone. He always maintained a positive enthusiastic "can-do" attitude. People were uplifted by his efforts. He never imposed an agenda on others. He never tried to impress others. He was a good listener and a loyal ally. He was also a good friend and a helpful neighbor. For instance, he noticed when the wind blew down a vacationing neighbor's large tree. When they returned it was cut into lengths and neatly stacked, all done anonymously.

Should Helpful Harry offer to take a neighbor boy fishing, parents would correctly be cautious because careful monitoring is always recommended. Such thoughtfulness parallels the superficially considerate behavior demonstrated by Groomers. When in doubt, erring on the side of caution is always best. Without further information, it is appropriate to prevent Helpful Harry from having unimpeded access to children. Closer scrutiny would reveal a number of differences between a truly thoughtful person such as Helpful Harry, and the manipulative grooming, masquerading as thoughtfulness, used by child molesters. Helpful Harry is not focused on gaining access to children. Even when parents declined the fishing invitation for their son he participated in their lives and remained a loyal and friendly ally. He never tickled and tussled with children. He was equally respectful of children as he was of adults. He was interested in their development, but remained interested in them as they matured into adults. He had a friendship with the parents, and because he was a loyal friend to them, he wanted to help them however he could. He was never focused on the children because they were children. He developed meaningful relationships, not superficial connections.

There was never the slightest hint of gossip, scandal, or controversy regarding his behavior with children. He never took liberties and never pushed the boundaries of appropriate privacy, personal space, or touch. He respected children, but never responded to them as a peer. He had a rich life, without obsessive needs to continuously be around children. He was respectful to children, but only interacted with children because of friendships with their families.

RECOGNIZING THE MANIPULATIVE

Helpful Harry truly cared about others. Slippery Sam only masqueraded as a thoughtful person. The differences between these two adults can become more clearly visible to those willing to look closely. This is another composite case to help the reader learn to differentiate between the truly helpful and those whose activities are intended to give them unimpeded access to children.

Slippery Sam

Slippery Sam was retired and spent his time volunteering at elementary schools. He spent time on the playgrounds, always with pounds of candy in his pockets. He organized games for children to find the candy on his person, including his pants' pockets. Everywhere he went he looked like the pied piper. Children eagerly followed him, hoping for candy, a tussle, or any other attention.

Parents adored him. They viewed his attention to the children as beneficial, but like cotton candy, his attentions lacked content. He volunteered at the school, but his involvement with children was superficial. While other volunteers helped students learn math skills or become more proficient readers, Slippery Sam spent his time engaged in play activities. He swung children on the swings, lifted them onto the monkey bars, or gave them candy, tickling them all the while. Children accustomed to his antics noted that when they were older he no longer remembered them. When school officials recommended he no longer pick up children or give them candy, he became enraged, and moved to a school where his manner was more appreciated.

Although Helpful Harry helped his friends, Slippery Sam only developed friendships because of his interest in children, and only provided the appearance of helpfulness. Helpful Harry developed relationships; Slippery Sam never retained connections with the families he mesmerized. In fact, he disappeared as soon as the children reached puberty, moving on to other families with younger children. Understanding the difference between Helpful Harry and Slippery Sam is crucial in protecting children from harm.

Groomer Profile

To summarize the items already discussed, the well-socialized child molesters described in this book exhibit a number of the following features. Well-socialized child molesters are

- Too helpful
- Too private
- Too attentive to children
- Too touchy with children
- Too involved with image management
- Too one-sided in relationships (always giving, never taking)
- Too opportunistic
- Too superficial
- Too prone to violate boundaries of personal space and privacy
- Too aggressive when confronted
- Too quick to drop friendships when children grow older
- Too likely to disappear when contact with children is denied
- Altogether too charming
- Too good to be true

Chapter 7

A Framework for Understanding
Child Sexual Abuse

THE UNDERLYING PATTERN

The trouble with child sexual abuse is that events that should be viewed as reflecting an enduring pattern of ongoing misconduct are instead seen individually, independently, and in isolation. Groomers evade detection because the overall pattern of their behavior remains invisible. Relevant pieces of information are available to various people who have known and lived with or worked with the Groomer, but this knowledge never reaches the authorities. Sometimes the clues are spread over large time periods, or are geographically far apart. Former spouses and girlfriends have their suspicions. Friends and neighbors had their complaints. Worried employers were relieved to see him leave, but never dared voice any possible suspicions in a letter of reference. Neighbors whose children were molested never pressed charges to spare their children from the further trauma of an investigation and publicity of a trial. Children who had previously been abused knew what happened but never told anyone. All these players remain silent. When allegations eventually arise none of these other prior victims learn of the accusations. Each continues to suffer alone.

This pattern of silence and isolation that usually occurs in these cases was briefly broken when Elizabeth Smart was abducted from her home in June 2002. Because the abduction became front-page news, former victims contacted the parents to reveal their suspicions about Brian Mitchell, who had been employed by the Smart family as a day laborer. Mitchell's ex-wife and her children talked directly to Elizabeth's parents, providing specific information about Mitchell's prior conduct. Unfortunately, in that particular case, the information shared by these two families—information that eventually resulted in

Elizabeth's return—was initially not adequately pursued by the investigating police, resulting in nine months of unnecessary suffering for all concerned. Child molesters do not operate in total secrecy and isolation; eventually many of the people who have known them become aware of their proclivities, but this knowledge too often remains untapped.

This was demonstrated in the cases discussed in this book: Parents worried about Marvelous Marvin's behavior, wondered whether they were overreacting, did not want to offend a friend or needlessly harm the reputation of a highly regarded community member, and agonized about how to proceed. Businessman Bob had already created a trail of consternation, as had Cranky Coach Carl and Dr. Dan. Such individualized agonizing and struggling occurs in every case, and at every level among those encountering the Groomers. Each individual who deals with the Groomer fails to benefit from knowing about prior difficulties. Each of the pieces of the puzzle, seen alone, fails to provide sufficient clarity or evidence to warrant lodging a formal complaint.

Just as individuals encountering child molesters operate alone and in isolation, organizations similarly isolate each complaint when complaints do arise. When parents complained about Coach Carl's conduct to the soccer league, the league dismissed each complaint, attributed behaviors to his "old-fashioned" coaching style, and made excuses for his conduct. In a small town where a teacher appeared to be sexually molesting the children, many parents independently went to the principal regarding concerns about the teacher's behavior. The principal handled each case as if there had never been any other prior complaints, each time assuring parents he would investigate the matter. Each complaint was followed by the principal reporting to the parents: "I talked to the teacher in question. Nothing happened. There is nothing to worry about. It's all a misunderstanding."

In the case of educator Robert Noyes, whose sexual assaults on students repeatedly came to the attention of school personnel in numerous communities, frightened and angry parents were placated every time. This continued for years until too many complaints were lodged, or the parents began talking to one another and approaching the principal in groups. Once the complaints become too overwhelming to ignore, or parents threatened to call the police, Noyes was transferred. He was sent to another school district, always with glowing recommendations to expedite the transfer, where he continued to molest students (van Dam, 2001). The pattern would be repeated in each new district, with every complaint viewed in isolation and each family whose children were being abused remaining ignorant of the fact that similar concerns had already been voiced in every district where this teacher had worked.

Similarly, Father Geoghan's sexual misconduct frequently came to the attention of the diocese. Complaints regarding sexual abuse continued in every location where he was transferred. The families in each new church, unaware of the prior problems, discovered anew the fears and anger previously experienced by many. In the process, hundreds of children continued to be molested because information known about his sexual proclivities was suppressed by higher church authorities who continued to transfer him to new and unsuspecting communities.

Precisely because activities surrounding child sexual abuse are seemingly invisible and occur in a domain uncomfortable for people to address directly, most of the information regarding sexual misconduct is never officially identified. The mishandling identified in the Catholic Church is what typically happens in child sexual abuse cases (van Dam, 2001). The Catholic Church does not have a monopoly on this mismanagement of the problem. Rather, in case after case extensive information is often known about the sexual misconduct. Parents of victims, the organizations that employ the alleged offender, and the family of the offender typically learn about some of the grooming techniques, boundary violations, odd behavior, or downright blatant sexual violations. However, no documentation exists to reveal this awareness, or track the accumulating evidence. Each informant operates alone and in a vacuum.

These patterns can be noted whenever grooming child molesters lurk in organizations responsible for managing youth. Exhaustive research investigations usually reveal the existence of prior suspicions or information regarding earlier sexual abuse allegations, or concerns about earlier sexual improprieties, information already known by many of the people surrounding the individual in question. By the time that Marvelous Marvin was volunteering his services at the church, a number of parents had stopped letting him babysit their children because of stories that included crawling into sleeping bags, showing his penis, and producing "white pee." The list grew to include more specific complaints such as forcing oral sex on a developmentally disabled boy, and anal sex on another boy. His church activities raised eyebrows because he constantly was seen accompanying children to the bathroom. None of this information was available to guide parents encountering Marvin for the first time.

This wealth of information remains invisible to police when asked to investigate. When parents complained to the police that Marvelous Marvin had forced anal sex on their developmentally disabled sixteen-year-old son, the police failed to understand the problem in the correct context, and never knew to look further. They viewed the case as not worth pursuing because the boy was sixteen, and Marvin was, after all, a good upstanding citizen. When another complaint was later made, this time that Marvin had forced anal sex on a young boy, the police ignored the prior information. Another officer investigated the new charge, and accepted Marvin's explanation because the officer was uncomfortable with the topic, was unaware Marvin's explanation is typically used by child molesters, and was also impressed with Marvin's sincerity.

When a child molester is eventually charged and convicted for a sexual offense, much of the information known about the perpetrator by those in the community who have witnessed improprieties remains obscured. As a result, none of this ongoing evidence regarding continuously risky behavior that should be incorporated in sentencing, treatment requirements, risk assessments, and parole planning is available to the officials who need it. These data need to be utilized to more quickly stop child molesters from molesting children, and more accurately differentiate between those who are dangerous from those whose behavior can be more safely managed. The evidence can then be used to more accurately predict risk and provide management recommendations for convicted child molesters upon release.

MAKING INFORMATION MORE VISIBLE

The following format is recommended to more clearly examine these phases of increasing awareness that occur in child sexual abuse cases. This framework delineates how behavior associated with child sexual abuse might initially seem invisible to the untrained eye, but can actually be utilized to more efficiently address public safety, as well as to manage risk. The task is to corral that information to help make it visible in a format useful for those in authority.

In some rare cases, a first sexual offense against a child may directly result in a conviction. The more typical cases reported in this book are based on thousands of child molesters who frequently acknowledge committing anywhere from a handful to thousands of sexual assaults that never result in any legal repercussions (Bolen, 2001; Cook, 1989; Salter, 2003). Such offenders cut a swath through the communities where they live, leaving behind them a trail of distraught, confused, and helpless people who have no information but their own small piece of the puzzle.

For the person with the untrained eye, child sexual abuse will appear to be a rare and shocking occurrence, occasionally reported in the media. Things look much different to experts who know the operating styles of these offenders. The offenders under discussion are so active, it is as if each child in the community has a swarm of offenders buzzing around them looking for an opportunity to molest. Aware parents may often seem paranoid because they might view interested adults as being potential offenders whereas naïve adults see only friendly and charming acquaintances. Perceptive and forewarned parents often note that the charmers they chased off were later revealed to be child molesters. Unfortunately, as can be seen in the case of the Catholic Church controversy, confirmation sometimes comes twenty years later. Since Groomers engage in suspicious behavior almost daily, significant information continuously accumulates.

HOW INFORMATION REMAINS BURIED

Currently this information is not available to the people who need it most for a number of reasons:

Nothing is ever reported: This was the case with Dr. Dan. Many different parents over the years were concerned about his conduct, his frequent desire to conduct impromptu invasive physical examinations, his regular use of rectal thermometers, and other problematical incidents. Each of the parents responded by removing their son from the activities or changing doctors, but no formal allegations or charges were ever made. Nothing appeared on society's radar.

The information is reported, but ignored, discounted, discredited, and therefore discarded: Over the years many parents complained about Coach Carl's behavior. He was seen "pantsing" children, patting them on the buttocks, and generally violating their personal space in ways that made both children and parents uncomfortable. When parents complained to the soccer league they were told that Coach Carl was an old-fashioned coach and "it doesn't mean anything. That's just his coaching style." The league became so used to these complaints that before new families ever met Coach Carl they were told not to worry. Nothing was ever said about the fact that two sexual misconduct allegations had been made to police in previous years. Since neither allegation led to an arrest or conviction, that information too vanished into thin air.

The information is actively suppressed by an organization to protect the organization's reputation and the good name of the alleged offender, and the police are never notified: This consistently occurred in the many cases of complaints about pedophile priests reported in the press (The Investigative Staff of *The Boston Globe,* 2002). This has also been seen in the mismanagement of similar cases by schools (van Dam, 2001). Typically, when enough parents begin to worry about a particular person's behavior they tend to voice their concerns to the organization employing the alleged offender, namely the school, the church, or the sports league, rather than dealing directly with the police. Staff at the church where Marvelous Marvin was volunteering did exactly that. They took their concerns to the church.

Typically, such organizations neither have personnel who are trained in conducting an investigation, nor should investigations ever be done internally, as the organization will inevitably come to the defense of the alleged offender and move into a "damage-control" mode. Once an organization takes such a stance, further information about possible misconduct by staff only more deeply locks them into a potentially wrong position, as the organization then begins to worry about lawsuits from both victims and accused alleged offenders.

*Earlier allegations or concerns that did not result in a convic-
tion are not investigated further when new allegations occur:*
Groomers benefit because investigators fail to seek historical
information and often miss opportunities for closer scrutiny
when complaints do arise. When the police were called to
Marvelous Marvin's house because of the complaints by
neighbors, the police witnessed a number of half-clad, very
young girls, and also observed that Marvin was serving alcohol to minors. Had they known about his past and chosen to
interview some of the party guests more closely, they would
have quickly learned about the sexual misconduct occurring
at that time. Instead, he was only charged with serving alcohol to minors and all evidence of possible sexual misconduct
was overlooked. Failure to incorporate all the evidence frequently occurs. As a result, in almost every closely studied
case of individuals eventually convicted of sexual misconduct, that conviction represents only the tip of the iceberg.

THE FRAMEWORK

Correctly understanding the dangers of well-socialized Groomers
under investigation requires knowing that much of the information
essential to differentiate those who are guilty from those who are
falsely accused can only be discovered by knowing to look "beyond
the tip of the iceberg." Only a thorough investigation by trained professionals will reveal the existence of a trail of slime. The iceberg
must be seen in its entirety.

THE ICEBERG

The "iceberg" metaphor reflects how little of the information
known about child molesters by various community members is ever
detected by the adults responsible for the safety of children. Even less
frequently does information about a given child molester reach the
authorities responsible for public safety. For example, the horizontal
line represents sea level. When information finally rises above that
level it becomes more public. Most of the evidence about child sexual

abuse, however, remains underwater, like an iceberg, invisible to the authorities.

In the case of Marvelous Marvin, many early indicators revealed his fixation on children. This, in combination with other clues, could have alerted people to watch more closely because those early activities paralleled behaviors typically used by child molesters. Although these clues alone would not have confirmed his sexual proclivities, additional information would correctly have been perceived as more significant had they been viewed in context. On the tip of the iceberg, Marvelous Marvin was convicted for one instance of sexual misconduct. Additional charges pending against him at that time were dropped. He had no other sexual criminal history.

THE ICEBERG

Risk Management in the Community
Release
Sexual conviction(s)
Pled down (sexual) conviction(s)
History of official charges and arrests

Allegations to Police That Do Not Result in Arrest
Complaints: To organizations, employers, or supervisors
Street Knowledge: community networking of friends and family
Shock and Disbelief: Innuendoes, suspicions, or observations
Secrecy: No overt awareness of possible child sexual abuse

Much of the information when examined in isolation does not warrant an arrest or conviction for sexual misconduct. The information is, however, indicative of high-frequency abusive behavior that continued to be ignored by police investigating subsequent complaints. Awareness of these patterns should have resulted in a more thorough police investigation when police responded to the complaint of Marvin's sexual contact with a developmentally delayed teenage boy, again when they next investigated the complaint about possible anal sex with another young boy, and again when they later investigated his party with half-dressed young girls. They also ignored the fact that Marvin had impregnated a thirteen-year-old girl. Each of these events should have resulted in interviews with parents, neighbors, and children. Furthermore, the therapist who counseled Marvin regarding the known earlier pregnancy failed to report the information to police as required by law. Such unprofessional conduct should not be ignored. Reporting requirements that are designed to protect children remain useless when not enforced.

One policeman familiar with Marvin's case at that time commented that he wanted to do a more thorough investigation. His supervisor told him, "We've got a conviction. We can't waste more time and money going after anything else." Correctly identifying the more extensive earlier evidence of ongoing sexual misconduct through extensive detective work would stop Groomers, like Marvin, long before they abuse hundreds of children. Instead, Marvelous Marvin said, "I found out I could get away with it. The police didn't even think this was such a big deal, so I figured it wasn't that bad. I didn't think I was hurting anyone, and the police obviously didn't mind or they would have done something about it."

Unfortunately, the Marvelous Marvins who get away with most of their sexual assaults are the rule rather than the exception. The research shows that only a very small percentage of offenses are ever identified or adjudicated. In each allegation that does occur, the lurid clues of ongoing sexual misconduct that should be used to more extensively guide investigations are instead ignored. As a result, each instance of possible sexual misconduct that leaks through at every level of the iceberg is examined in isolation. Victims, families, organizations, and communities therefore continue to be subjected to the predatory behavior of socially skilled Groomers without benefiting from any of that prior information.

Known information at each level of the iceberg should be revealed to help direct interventions and investigations, as well as to manage community safety. In case after case, however, the rich information known by the various community members struggling individually with the Groomer remains unknown to the decision makers assessing, treating, and supervising even identified child molesters. As a result, these important tasks, intended to protect the community, incorporate only a small fraction of information visible "above the water." To better understand this framework, a closer look at each layer of the iceberg will be helpful.

discuss use of Private Detector

The Base: Total Secrecy

Individuals, organizations, and communities stuck at this level are naïve to the operating practices of Groomers. This makes their children more vulnerable to child molesters.

People may assume that child sexual abuse, by its nature, is secret. Certainly there are many instances where no one other than the victim and the assailant are aware of the sexual contact. More often, people suspect something to be amiss, but discount their intuition, assume they are overreacting, or talk themselves out of it (van Dam, 2001; de Becker, 1999). In fact, most parents recall with 20/20 hindsight the clues that revealed something to have been wrong. This was true for Wanda, as she remembered that long before her daughter finally disclosed, she had been uncomfortable with Bob's attention to this daughter. Despite her discomfort, she assumed everything was fine because she was sure her daughter would tell if anything were happening.

Similarly, in the case of Dr. Dan, no one was initially aware of any sexual misconduct. The amount of time he spent with young boys, and the extent of his socialization with them to the exclusion of his other commitments might have raised red flags, but information regarding any sexual misconduct was technically invisible. A few young boys knew what was happening, but many of them kept the secret. Had adults been aware of the grooming practices used by socially skilled child molesters, Dr. Dan's behavior would have looked worrisome enough to suggest the need for distancing children from him, but would not have provided evidence to confirm that children were being sexually abused. Some of the boys revealed a few distinctly odd practices to their parents, who believed their sons and removed them from any continued contact with Dr. Dan. Since these parents did nothing further to reveal their information to anyone else, nothing more could be done.

The secrecy of the abuse allows it to flourish, which ensures that many children are harmed. Since most child molesters first charm adults to secure access to children, informed parents would be less likely to welcome and tolerate the attentions Groomers direct toward them and their children. Informed adults know not to expect children to protect themselves from abuse, and recognize no one is above suspicion. Therefore, in addition to teaching children to be assertive, encouraging them to disclose inappropriate conduct, and being able to hear such information, they also learn to more directly protect children from harm by becoming educated on the topic.

Most Groomers tend to be incredibly charming and extremely helpful, and direct their activities for gaining admission into homes, organizations, or communities where children congregate. Just like a salesman may charm a prospective customer to close a sale, or a politician would be disarming to get a vote, these child molesters often also appear "too good to be true." Adults should be suspicious of someone who prefers the company of children, tends to be childlike in his play, frequently engages children in roughhousing or tickling activities, and somehow immediately becomes a close and trusted friend. In fact, when Groomers find that efforts to enchant fail to provide immediate access to children, they slip away, as their intent is to spend time with children, not socialize with adults (van Dam, 2001). The speed of their disappearance when efforts to gain access to children fail suggests their motives may have been problematical.

To prevent such potential child molesters from having any opportunities to molest, adults must establish clear boundaries regarding acceptable conduct, and worry when such boundaries are ignored or ridiculed. Parents who set dietary restrictions for their children, whether for health or religious reasons, expect friends and family to abide by those restrictions. Supposedly well-meaning friends who independently decide, "Oh, a few chocolates won't really hurt," are not respecting parental boundaries. This may seem like a trivial point, but it is the parent's prerogative. Whereas true friends respect boundaries, opportunistic child molesters not only ignore boundaries, but when confronted they tend to go on the offensive. Individuals whose conduct parallels behaviors used by offenders need never be proven to be a child molester. Parents need only disengage from relationships with such individuals.

Adults who understood this perspective were not charmed by Marvelous Marvin, but found his behavior odd: They wondered why a teenager would prefer socializing with children. They could not understand why he would buy a van equipped with toys for children instead of the type of car most boys his age covet. They might not have known that he was a child molester, but they found his motives suspicious. Thus, while much of the information about Marvelous Marvin's conduct might technically have been secret, the behavioral pattern already was predictable enough to have caused concern.

Level Two: Shock and Disbelief

Individuals, organizations, and communities stuck at this level are aware child molesters exist, but lack of knowledge and continued isolation leave them immobilized. If level one is the willful ignorance of people and/or communities in denial, level two is about the grief, anger, pain, confusion, fear, and frustration accompanying the collapse of ignorant bliss.

Considering the possibility that someone known, loved, and trusted might sexually harm children is so unpleasant that most adults cannot believe it to be possible, which can make them blind to clues. Minor clues may be visible but are only *later* understood. So often, after abuse has been identified, parents remember the slight discomforts they experienced but never attributed to possible abuse. Typically heard are such remarks as:

- "I didn't like the way that he looked at my daughter."
- "I felt it was really odd how he was always hanging out with so many boys. It didn't seem possible that he could have that much free time during the day since he had a full-time job."
- "I thought it was weird that he had so many kids around, and that he always had kids over for the night."
- "I was uncomfortable with the presents he was buying for her."

Because it is so difficult to believe that an admired, loved, or respected friend, family member, or professional would sexually molest children, most adults respond to information about possible sexual misconduct with shock and disbelief. Because the alternatives are too frightening, they attribute any possible allegations of sexual misconduct to being a "misunderstanding," an "error in judgment," or that "it didn't really mean anything." The more successful, respected, loved, or feared the alleged perpetrator is, the more likely the adults dealing with that offender remain stuck at this level.

Many parents who knew Marvelous Marvin experienced discomfort about his behavior, or heard comments that seemed odd. Similar concerns surrounded Dr. Dan. One mother found it peculiar that her young son needed to disrobe to have his ear examined, and another mother felt uncomfortable that her son's sore throat required an anal swab. Both mothers discounted their discomfort because Dr. Dan was a respected and successful doctor. In every case, concerns were suppressed and nothing further was done. Had these parents understood how child molesters operate they might have had the courage to look more closely and might have given greater credence to their discomfort. Had they participated in a supportive community network, they might have more readily known what to do with their information. Although, often there is insufficient information at this stage to lodge any formal complaints to the police.

The reaction of shock and disbelief is normal with emotionally difficult news. Kübler-Ross refers to the first stage of grief as denial (1969). Prochaska and colleagues prefer to use the term "precontemplation" as a way to indicate someone is not yet ready to take action guaranteed to be difficult (1994). Summit describes it as nescience (1989). In any event, at this stage the individual maintains an "ostrich-head-in-the-sand" approach to stave off overwhelming grief and/or guaranteed difficulty should suspicions be credited.

Many remain stuck at this stage for a number of reasons: The available information can always seem vague and incomplete, the alleged offender will always go to great lengths to allay any concerns, and knowing what to do next is unclear and scary. As a result, people often may prefer to either discredit allegations of sexual abuse, claim victims fabricate stories for secondary gain, or fault therapists for creating false memories among clients who were never victims of sexual assault. Denial provides a secure insulation, avoiding the need for uncomfortable action.

Others may avoid considering the possibility of sexual abuse because it could jeopardize the status quo. They disbelieve children in order to keep the security provided by the working spouse whose conduct has been questioned. Some may remain in this state of denial even after the alleged offender has been convicted, continuing to accept the child molester's version of reality despite all evidence to the contrary. For most independent thinkers, remaining at this stage becomes increasingly difficult as more damning evidence begins to filter through.

Even when the adults give credence to the possibility that something happened, considering that someone known, loved, and trusted might have committed abuse does not automatically start an official investigation. The available information always seems tenuous and confusing, and as a result, often nothing is done or can be done given the current system. The adult who acknowledges that something happened, but has nothing sufficient to warrant calling the police, will typically have no other recourse but to do nothing. Even when asked the hypothetical question of how they would respond in such a situation, many adults would do nothing for fear of unnecessarily harming an upstanding citizen. Furthermore, supportive parents of children who have been sexually abused are not eager to see their children being made to testify at trial, worrying about the additional trauma.

When children do tell, they usually minimize what happened because it is embarrassing or frightening. One convicted child molester remarked, "my victims, when asked, would tell. But they never told even one half of one percent of what happened." With direct questioning, one child this offender routinely sodomized admitted, "he touched me once," an admission obtained only after lengthy direct questioning by an adult who was certain the child had been abused. Since children are also often threatened by the offender, told they and their family will be harmed, or reminded by the offender that any disclosure will destroy the family, disclosures, when they do occur, might be indirect or incomplete.

One child told her mother "I don't like my teacher. He's always tickling me." The mother eventually learned the tickling "is under my shirt," which she understood to be incorrect behavior on the part of the teacher. She did not know what to do about this information. She had taught her child about "good touch, bad touch," and had encouraged her child to tell if anyone touched her in "the bad way," but "I just didn't know what to make of this. It didn't seem like sexual abuse." Though she credited the information, and was concerned about what might be happening, she did not know what should be done.

Adults learning about possible misconduct who are at this stage realize that something inappropriate may have taken place, and are ready to consider the possibility that a known, trusted, or loved person might have misbehaved. However, because the information is vague and confusing, they do not know what to do, and therefore often do nothing.

Marvelous Marvin generated a number of vague disclosures from many of the children he molested. One little girl described not liking being scrubbed in the tub. Another boy did not like spending so much time in the bathroom. One girl wondered why Marvin's "pee pee" was so big. None of these children provided more information. Their parents each terminated contact with Marvin, but did not know what else should be done.

This same confusion surrounded Dr. Dan: One boy wanted to quit the baseball team Dr. Dan coached. His mother knew he loved the game. He was the star pitcher, which made his desire to quit more difficult to understand. When she asked why, he only said he did not like the medical examinations, but when asked for clarification, he clammed up.

Often adults might feel they cannot terminate contact with the alleged perpetrator, so instead decide, "I'll just keep a closer eye on things." They assume such closer scrutiny will prevent anything further from occurring. Unfortunately, however, many child molesters enjoy the added challenge of molesting children in the presence of adults. One offender boasted,

> I even jacked off their six-year-old son right there in the living room. We were all watching a movie. The little boy was sitting on my lap under a blanket, like he always does. He even squealed with delight, and they didn't notice a thing. Why would they? I was their friend.

Most people find this inconceivable, but in fact "It only takes a second to sexually molest a child" (Halliday-Sumner, 1997).

At this level, only a trickle of the information reflecting what has really happened has bubbled up this far, but the adults who reach this level of awareness accept the possibility something might be amiss. Once they recognize that there is a possible problem, they might recollect small details, inconsistencies, and alarms they had previously ignored, which in light of the disclosures become more meaningful. However, they still do not know what to do, and typically are not sure whether what happened would constitute sexual abuse. Parents report, "We weren't sure what it was. All we were told was a little touching down the shirt." As a result, they still do nothing.

Level Three: Street Knowledge

Individuals, organizations, and communities operating at this level recognize child molesters exist. They cannot believe the people they know and love could be child molesters.

In case after case of the Groomers studied, their behavior left a trail of confusion and speculation. For many of the families, the information, questions, and concerns generated by the molesters was initially kept quiet, leaving each new group to encounter the child molester alone without awareness of any of the prior problems.

As the number of assaults increase, the clues begin stacking up. In case after case, more information eventually bubbles to the surface in casual conversations between friends, parents, neighbors, and acquaintances. A mother worrying about Marvelous Marvin's odd behavior mentioned it to another mother during a soccer game. Two parents chatting during a baseball game began talking about Dr. Dan. A number of parents started talking about their concerns regarding Coach Carl while watching their boys play soccer.

Once parents suspect something has happened, but do not know what should be done, there is a natural building of alliances and consultation between friends, neighbors, colleagues, and sometimes professionals. These discussions frequently uncover similar concerns by others because of the high level of activity typically associated with socially skilled Groomers. Such discussions generate a better understanding that something is definitely amiss.

One mother described her daughter's comment about "Marvin's pee pee" to a friend. The friend responded that her son was unhappy with the amount of time Marvelous Moving Marvin forced him to spend in the bathroom. Both mothers were surprised to not be alone in their concerns, as they assumed "everybody loves Marvin." Overhearing these two mothers, another parent added, "I heard some kids saying, "Marvin's pee is white." Another mother knew Marvin had impregnated a thirteen-year-old girl. "She was sent out of town for an abortion, and Marvin was supposed to get therapy." The individual pieces of information that appeared so ambiguous but sinister when viewed in isolation became even more frightening when the other stories were shared.

Similarly, information about Dr. Dan began leaking out. The mother whose son no longer wanted to play baseball happened to mention her son's discontent to her neighbor. The neighbor responded that her son said he no longer wanted to go cross-country skiing with Dr. Dan, because "Dr. Dan always wants to talk about why I am not circumcised. I don't like it." As a result of this conversation, both mothers began talking to more friends. One mother recalled her son saying he did not like Dr. Dan because "he's always wanting to do a medical examination." Another boy told his mother he was uncomfortable with the way Dr. Dan, before any outing, required taking his temperature with a rectal thermometer. Another mother noticed her son avoided Dr. Dan, and that he became hysterical whenever he needed a sports physical. None of the mothers knew what to do, but after talking to one another decided to take action.

In other words, what typically happens is that the continuing activity of the well-socialized child molester eventually raises so many questions and concerns that the resulting wake of innuendoes, clues, activities, and questions reach a crescendo that eventually can no longer be ignored. In talking to thousands of child molesters, hundreds of community members, and the different families encountering this problem, these discussions occur because of the continuous predatory activities typical of the Groomers. Although, after being convicted once, Marvelous Moving Marvin discovered the best way to avoid further detection was to leave town "about every five years before anybody has a chance to figure it out and try to bust me." This is a technique Bottom-feeder Buddy had perfected early in his offending career.

Talking to others provides helpful information. This is how health professionals staff cases. This is also how parents relay important facts regarding numerous concerns about child development and health. For example, they learn from one another that temper tantrums in two-year-olds may be normal, or be solaced knowing everyone else has similar experiences. They learn a rash might be an allergic reaction, a fever symptomatic of a recent virus, or benefit from the experiences of mothers whose children have already been through that developmental stage. They discover other parents are equally stymied by the same problems. Parents communicate with one another about the trials and tribulations of raising children, while sharing the joys and excitement, and trading helpful hints and useful parenting strategies, often doing this while cheering their children on during a sports activity, or when volunteering at various school or church events.

Women are more likely than men to process concerns (Gilligan, 1992; Pipher, 1996). Significant differences exist between how women talk to one another and how men talk with one another. Women are more likely to talk about personal concerns, anxieties, and other details about daily life

(Gilligan, 1992). This was recently exemplified when a husband attended a reunion of fishing buddies, and, despite a week of socializing, never learned that one of them was separated from his spouse. When his wife joined them shortly thereafter, she immediately learned about the pending divorce from the other wives. When she asked her husband how he could not have known, he said, "It just never came up." The men talked about fish, boats, motors, the weather on the ocean, and other "important" things. For the wife to instantly learn about the pending divorce is not gossip, but rather sharing information, thereby strengthening the social network.

This type of talk differs from gossip in a number of ways: (1) it is not malicious; (2) it is intended to help process information, debrief events, and educate; and (3) it includes sharing personal stories, revealing one's own predicaments and worries, and therefore becomes both therapeutic and educational. This is also how newcomers to a community more efficiently access various services for their children. This parallels how health professionals staff cases. By sharing social information and issues, women also tend to provide warning information regarding people whose behavior seems problematical. On this basis, for instance, neighbors told a new neighbor why they would not use another neighbor girl as a babysitter, or recommended the services of one doctor over another. Mothers trade information about teachers constantly. By doing this they are able to steer their children away from notoriously incompetent teachers, using whatever influence they can muster with school authorities to benefit from those teachers with the best reputations. They pass on the information making the rounds, adding data of their own. In this way, community members no longer rely only on tip-of-the-iceberg data, but begin looking beneath the water as best they can.

The child molesters under discussion are continuously seeking the next opportunity to molest. This goal-directed behavior generates a flurry of activity that requires ongoing contacts with more adults and opportunities for access to more children. As a result, the offenders that remain in the same community create increased evidence of wrongdoing, leading to ever more opportunities for people to worry about their conduct and have information to share with friends and neighbors. Unfortunately, however, most of the information available to these individuals never rises above the water level and therefore never becomes incorporated into investigations or subsequent prison risk assessments that generate treatment or release management recommendations.

Offenders commonly change jobs or towns when a place "gets too hot." Many different types of criminals do this once they become too well-known by the local authorities. In the case of child molesters, however, it is not enough for parents to feel relief when a suspected offender moves to another town, stops coaching a specific team, or agrees to voluntarily stop teaching. This is because the offender will begin grooming a new community of unsuspecting adults, enjoying a clean slate while new children are harmed by abuse. Adults owe it to children to remain involved in protecting all children from harm from these well-socialized successful Groomers.

Level Four: Complaints Made

Individuals, organizations, and communities operating at this level recognize trusted individuals can be child molesters. They do not understand the addictive nature of child sexual abuse. Instead, they believe or hope the problems can be managed internally.

Finally, when suspicions and events reach "critical mass," someone finally lodges a complaint. Sometimes the complaint is made directly to the suspected offender. Marvin described how on a number of occasions "I would have this talk." A friend would say to him "I want you to stop what you're doing to my kid." When these confrontations occurred, "I would just sit and listen. Usually, they would talk themselves out of it. They just didn't want to believe that I would do these things." After such a talk, "I would sometimes stop. More often, however, I would just be more careful." Over the years a number of parents also geared themselves up to "confront" Coach Carl, who knew that things would "blow over" soon enough. These parents would leave and new, younger, unsuspecting children would join the team.

More typically, if the suspicions are not discussed directly with the offender, the initial complaints are made to an organization rather than directly to the police or state child protective services: Parents worried about a coach's behavior will eventually contact the sports league. Adults worrying about a teacher's behavior typically complain to the principal. Parishioners concerned about a priest or cleric talk to church authorities Complaints are typically not made to the police for a number of reasons: not being sure anything wrong really happened, not wanting to harm the reputation of a fine citizen, not being certain there is enough information to warrant an investigation, not wanting to make such a "private" matter public.

More often, people report being confused and uncertain, wanting to do something to protect children, but not really clear about what should be done.

- "We weren't sure what to call it. It was just touching under the shirt."
- "We didn't want to ruin the reputation of such a nice man."
- "I wasn't sure if it was sexual abuse."
- "I just wanted the problem to stop. I didn't want to hurt his career."
- "I thought he could get help for his problem."

Just as offenders note how parents "talk themselves out of it," organizations are equally unsuited to investigate allegations for a number of reasons:

1. They are not trained investigators. As a result, when complaints are first made they may collegially discuss the concerns with the accused. They subsequently accept an explanation with relief, and assume the matter to be over.
2. New complaints, should they arise, are then handled afresh and out of context.
3. Organizations begin to worry about liability. They fear lawsuits from the employee, and they fear lawsuits from the complaining parents.

This pattern occurs in case after case, as witnessed by hundreds of stories told by community members, parents, and organizations (Willmsen & O'Hagan, 2003; Zeeck, 2003). This same pattern also allowed the Catholic Church to continue protecting priests whose misconduct should have been reported to police (The Investigative Staff of *The Boston Globe*, 2002).

In one community, a young boy learning about good touch/bad touch from his mother, said, "You mean, like Mr. Clay?" his second grade teacher. The stunned mother discovered from her son that Mr.

Clay had also fondled a number of other boys in the classroom. Long discussions occurred between the five families whose sons had been identified as potential victims. The parents each talked to their own children to confirm the information, and together took their complaints to the principal. The principal responded by saying he would look into the matter. He talked to Mr. Clay who said, "Nothing happened." The principal therefore considered the matter closed (van Dam, 2001).

This story was also repeated with convicted child molester Robert Noyes during the first years of his teaching career. In every school district, parents of abused students complained to the principals. The principal would assure them that nothing had happened, or the problem was being dealt with. After too many complaints, Mr. Noyes would be transferred to another school district where everyone was unaware of his sexual proclivities (Halliday-Sumner, 1997).

In the case of Dr. Dan, a number of people lodged complaints. The sports league received a few phone calls from worried parents. The league responded to each case individually, arguing "nothing like this had ever come up before," he was an excellent coach who was well liked, and there was nothing to worry about. A few other parents contacted the medical association. They were told that he was a doctor in good standing, and were assured that they must have misunderstood the medical condition the doctor was examining. There was nothing to worry about. In each case, the adult making the call was nervous about even lodging a complaint, assumed the organization knew best, and let the matter drop.

At this stage the adults have sufficient information that they decide there is a need to take some action. They do not, however, feel comfortable reporting the information to the police because they do not have anything concrete to allege, do not wish their child to become involved in an investigation, and do not believe a criminal investigation is warranted. As a result, they choose to informally discuss the problem with the organization in charge of the person whose conduct they suspect.

Once the complaint is made at this level, the agency involved takes on its own investigation, which so easily ends up looking more like a cover-up. One school board member publicly boasted she finally learned how to successfully manage the parents, stating, "They really only want to ventilate and be placated. I don't have to do anything. I just let them vent, say some sympathetic words, and they go away satisfied." This approach summarizes how organizations often manage complaints. In other words, they all-too-often graciously placate the complainer, but *do nothing*. Organizations that work with children often view parents as prima donnas who make unreasonable demands, which may occur, but is an error they cannot afford to make. Once the organization fails to properly address the first complaint, they become entrenched in continuing to placate the parents while supporting the employee. With each new complaint they become more locked into pursuing the initial course of action.

As a result, often the information available to organizations regarding such complaints remains buried at this level. Once again, the information known by various people never bubbles above the surface and remains invisible during any subsequent investigation or conviction and therefore fails to also be incorporated when determining likelihood of guilt, appropriate sentencing, treatment, future risk, or ongoing management. In fact, because the court system never learned about any of the earlier evidence of sexual misconduct by Businessman Bob, and was therefore unaware that he was continuing to engage in exactly the same grooming and abuse behavior, he was not correctly identified as dangerous and his conduct remained under the radar.

Level Five: Allegations to Police

Individuals, organizations, and communities recognize that well-liked and respected individuals are capable of sexually abusing children. They know to take complaints directly to the police.

The scurry of activity surrounding these Groomers typically involves many increasingly suspicious people, yet no official record reflects these complaints or observations. With each new instance, and every new person encountering the misbehavior for the first time, most people find it very difficult to be certain enough that their problems merit calling the police. As already noted, they more typically assume events to be a "misunderstanding" or an "error in judgment." Often, they will address their complaint directly to the person whose behavior appeared suspect. As Marvelous Marvin pointed out, however, on the number of occasions that friends broached this topic with him they would invariably describe how much they valued his friendship, and then would ask him to refrain from doing anything to their children again. They "would talk themselves out of" any misgivings they had, and the relationship he had with their children would eventually continue as it had before. Only three times did an adult have sufficiently disturbing and detailed information that they complained directly to the police. Twice he convinced the police nothing happened. The third time he accepted the one charge in order to mask his other behavior, which by then had included molesting over 200 children.

In the case of Dr. Dan, one family went to the police. The young boy involved had not been one of Dr. Dan's primary targets. Rather, this boy had accompanied his cousin on a camping outing with Dr. Dan but had never before met the man. He participated in everything, from campfire tales of terror to snuggling in the tent after dark. When they were all in the tent, Dr. Dan "accidentally" molested the newcomer in the dark. Dr. Dan explained, "I thought it was Jimmy, my main friend. After I realized my mistake it was too late." The new boy immediately told his parents exactly what happened. These parents had no relationship with Dr. Dan, were scandalized, and reported directly to the police. For the first time the authorities were involved. The police had a brief talk with Dr. Dan, were assured that it had been a misunderstanding, and nothing further was done nor was any record of the accusation kept. Dr. Dan's victim grooming failed him that night, but his grooming of the community saved him.

By the time the police are contacted regarding Groomers, in all likelihood there have already been multiple incidents, many victims, and community awareness that something is amiss. The cases most likely to be immediately reported to the police or state child protective services (CPS) involve offenders who are less emotionally or financially secure, and less well entrenched in the community. Offenders like Bottom-feeder Buddy, should he remain in the community long enough, would be much more likely to be caught. Given his propensity to leave town, the number of times he has come to the attention of the authorities would be seen as surprisingly high compared to the other more emotionally sophisticated offenders described in this book.

The more well established the alleged offender might be, the more difficult it becomes for people to even consider reporting their concerns to the police. In most of these cases, by the time the police are involved a more thorough investigation would be expected to reveal much more than is indicated by the complaint alone, as was already evident with Businessman Bob, Marvelous Marvin, Dr. Dan, and Cranky Coach Carl.

Levels Six Through Nine: Arrests, Convictions, Sentencing, and Release Planning

Individuals, organizations, and communities know the individual has molested at least once. Knowledge, collaboration, and networking become crucial to avoid having known child molesters continue molesting children. Communities need to learn how to be vigilant without becoming vigilantes.

Predictable Peter was finally convicted for the first time as an old man, after having sexually molested his granddaughter. Based on the official record, this was the first and only offense committed by an upstanding citizen. Family and friends knew otherwise. Had anyone interviewed his daughters and their many friends, multiple incidents of sexual assaults against children would have been identified. None of that long pattern of sexual misconduct was included in the file, and therefore, information about Peter was based on the legal record only, namely one incident of child sexual abuse.

Businessman Bob had been convicted once for sexually molesting his daughter, which officially identified him as an "incest offender," and therefore he was viewed as being in the lowest-risk category regarding further offenses. He had ostensibly spent many years before that living in the community without any legal problems, although a closer investigation of his prior behavior would have revealed numerous girlfriends who all had young daughters, and a number of times when these relationships ended precisely because of concerns by the girlfriends regarding his behavior toward their young daughters. None of this information was contained in any of the official records, and thus he was identified as being a first-time incest offender when he was convicted for molesting his daughter. He subsequently remarried a woman who had two daughters, once again repeating a behavior pattern that should have been viewed as worrisome. He not only created a house that was a pleasure dome for his new stepdaughters, but encouraged them to invite their friends over, and successfully began proceedings to regain custody of his own younger daughters. Officially, Businessman Bob had one conviction for sexually molesting his daughter.

When a complaint is made to the police or child protective services, officials do their own investigation to determine whether the allegations are credible. This is the first point for the authorities to become involved. The police and courts in some communities have greater training and experience in these matters, and the result is reflected in the conviction records (van Dam, Halliday, & Bates, 1985). As more and more professionals continue to become better trained in the investigation methods needed to more effectively manage these types of cases, and learn to investigate these cases more carefully, they will need to consider expanding their investigations to talk to other community members who have previously known or lived with the person under investigation.

Typically, when a complaint is made, the investigation includes interviewing the alleged offender, as well as interviewing the person making the complaint and the child alleging the abuse. The problems are multiple, as offenders are often socially skilled and very adept at handling themselves in an investigation, while the victim is typically afraid and embarrassed.

Rarely do investigators tend to obtain any other corroborating data, and even more rarely would the rich history of innuendo and information known by prior neighbors, friends, or family ever be incorporated into the investigation. This can often be due to budget constraints, but is just as likely a limitation due to lack of understanding of the dynamics involved. In one custody case, the evaluator wanted to interview adults who had been children during an alleged molester's prior marriage. He contacted one daughter who confirmed being molested by her father when she was little, a call that should have been made by investigators. The evaluator was subsequently unable to convince the courts to open up an investigation, thereby ensuring the new custody concerns failed to take prior important information into account. Instead, the courts assigned another evaluator to the case.

Typically investigations are limited to the most recent allegations. If the investigating police consider there to be insufficient information to press charges, no further record of the allegation or the investigation is kept. This is unfortunate. Patterns of multiple allegations should be viewed as significant, but instead, remain invisible. Although in a democratic society a citizen is innocent until proven guilty, this does not mean child molesters who have not yet been convicted should have access to children. Nor does it mean that a convicted but "recovered" child molester can enjoy all rights and privileges, namely continued access to children.

Arrest

If the preliminary investigation reveals sufficient data to warrant that the abuse did occur, the individual will be arrested and accorded the rights and privileges of a trial. Some offenders admit guilt to a portion of what took place, which means that if they do not have a significant prior criminal record they become eligible for SSOSA, or Special Sex Offender Disposition Alternative (SSODA) if they are adolescents, thereby potentially avoiding a prison sentence altogether. This is exactly what Businessman Bob did. By admitting to molesting his daughter he was assured outpatient treatment, and felt confident the authorities would not conduct a closer examination of his other activities. For a number of offenders who deny culpability, the investigation reveals insufficient information to take the case to trial, and the matter is then dropped. In other cases, the arrest does lead to a trial.

Plea Bargaining

A number of offenders plead guilty to a much lesser charge in order to avoid the trial, and in the hopes of thereby minimizing the consequences. Marvelous Marvin managed this on two occasions: He ruefully admitted to having a drinking problem when the police found him surrounded by teenagers and alcohol. Then, with the later rape charge, he described his response as an "academy-award-winning performance," admitting to the one rape at trial, but insisting "I won't admit to something I haven't done," thereby avoiding the other charges. More commonly, a molestation will appear on the record as an assault, as frequently occurred to Bottom-feeder Buddy. Thus, the final conviction frequently does not accurately reflect what truly occurred.

Conviction

Businessman Bob's one conviction minimized much of what he had actually done to his daughter. Marvelous Marvin accepted the one rape conviction, having thereby avoided closer scrutiny on all his other sexually abusive activities. Predictable Peter avoided detection all his life, finally being convicted for the first time at the age of seventy. Most of the child molesters who fit the profile described in this book, if they are finally convicted, acknowledge a much more extensive history of molesting children than would ever be indicated by their convictions.

Release Planning

Once someone is convicted of a sex offense, determinations regarding their return to the community are eventually made. Such individuals might initially have two or three years of community supervision during which time there would be somewhat closer scrutiny over their conduct before they are free of any further supervision. Even child molesters who have to keep reporting their address to local police long after their probationary period is over can resume having unimpeded access to children.

Once free, Businessman Bob returned to the community and influenced the courts to give him custody of his younger daughters. Marvelous Moving Marvin chose to leave the state, learning to protect himself by never remaining in any one place long enough to come to the attention of the criminal justice system. Bottom-feeder Buddy has always been off the usual radar screens because he is homeless and has never worked. Some of the women whose children he molested never even knew his real name, nor would they know where to find him when he left, leaving him free to continue to meet unsuspecting women with daughters.

Chapter 8

Interviewing Child Molesters

As already noted, child molesters lie. They lie to themselves, and they lie to others. They lie even when they know their audience has direct access to the truth. They lie with such blatant ease, such good effect, and are so accustomed to having their lies accepted, that they lose track of the truth. Marvelous Marvin denied having impregnated the young teenage girl. It remained a mystery, and when DNA testing was threatened he enthusiastically supported the idea. "I know only something like that will help clear my name. I never touched her, and the test will prove it." His eager cooperation with testing finally had the hapless parents decide; "Oh, that's not necessary. We believe you." Businessman Bob similarly convincingly assured parents he had never touched their young developmentally delayed girl who accused him. His careful concern about her well-being falsely convinced them of his innocence.

As a group, Groomers tend to be extremely self-centered or narcissistic. This is to be expected as only someone with narcissistic tendencies can assume a child would be interested in sexual interactions with him or her. Only someone with narcissistic tendencies can presume that children desire his or her sexual attentions. Only such narcissism allows Groomers to sincerely mistake a child's normal behavior as a sexual invitation. "I knew she wanted it, the way she wriggled her butt at me and was always dropping her diaper around me." Only a person with narcissistic tendencies could fail to interpret the various ways in which children communicate displeasure, fear, and pain as meaning yes.

These narcissistic tendencies are often slightly masked by the ability of many of these child molesters to focus on the adults with whom they associate, whose children they hope to molest. Thus, they cater to the universal desire to be appreciated, and by recognizing the adults to be brilliant, perceptive, and thoughtful, they more efficiently ensure a quick acceptance into the fold. This strategy, noted among the "closet narcissists" (Masterson, 1988), allows them to enjoy the indirect glory while ensuring access to the children.

Although as a group child molesters tend to be extremely hypervigilant, this attentiveness is exclusive to only the information that would increase opportunity and access to children with ensured security. Thus, they are very observant of minute cues, noting exactly how to appear attentive to those adults responsible for children, picking up the slightest nuances that will help them gain access or maintain their security. This same attentiveness, however, often ensures that they miss and/or misunderstand many of the other nuances necessary for social interactions or normal intimacy with adults.

The very nature of the disorder can be successfully used in interviews with child molesters to obtain a better, more thorough understanding of their history, their cognitive distortions, and the details of their misconduct. Thus, the following recommendations are useful in investigating child molester cases, or conducting clinical interviews with child molesters. These same concepts are recommended for also better understanding the potential danger of being targeted by a child molester that all community members face who have responsibility and/or access to children.

The charm Groomers direct toward adults responsible for children is used to protect them from discovery, and also is used to good effect when they are questioned. Maintaining clarity and listening carefully are always challenging when talking to this population, but informed adults are more likely to identify the lies, inconsistencies, and deceit used by child molesters if they know what to expect.

These recommendations will help readers know how to be attentive. Remember, however, that investigations should be left to trained professionals. There is no need for community members to become vigilantes. However, responsible adults should ensure the greatest safety for children. Furthermore, the best decision for protecting children is: "When in doubt, do not provide unsupervised access." For those who fit the profile, graciously restricting access to children is the first line of defense.

Key concerns when interviewing child molesters include the following:

- Identifying lies
  —Admitting small errors
  —Creating distractions
- Phony remorse

- Creating relationship
- Inconsistencies
- Rehearsed speech
- Too much information
- Going on the offensive

IDENTIFYING LIES

Paying close attention allows the listener to better notice lies that might otherwise incorrectly be ignored as misunderstandings. Careful attention is needed to recognize when the information provided is at variance with fact, is inconsistent, or changes the topic altogether. Lies usually work for child molesters for a number of reasons. Most people assume that everyone around them tells the truth about most things. Child molesters often lie about everything. By lying, and discovering that they can get away with little lies, they learn who to target, and therefore whose children to target. As one mother noted, after discovering that the man she had been married to for years had been molesting all of her daughters, "I used to believe he lied about some things and told the truth about most things. Now I realize he lied about most things and hardly ever told the truth."

Lying also allows child molesters to more effectively and efficiently create whatever image they wish to present, as well as to remain in control of the conversation. Thus, they lie to friends and to family members, they lie to police when they are being interrogated, and they lie on the stand when they are questioned. They continue to lie even after they have been incarcerated, minimizing what happened, or remaining quiet about most of the events that were never identified.

Marvelous Marvin exemplified this when he described the sexual assault that finally resulted in his first conviction, when the girl reported the rape and medical evidence confirmed it. "I admitted what I had done and I was charged with one count of first-degree rape." However, despite the fact that police finally interviewed some of the other children surrounding him, which led to his being charged with five other counts, there was only strong evidence on one count. As a result, Marvelous Marvin admitted to the rape, "but I got very self-righteous and said, 'I won't admit to something I haven't done.' And I denied all the other charges. They bought that," which meant that he was able to avoid a prison sentence and instead became a candidate for SSOSA.

Each of the offenders described in this book, who should be viewed as representative of many of the child molesters living in the community, used various innumerable lies and distortions to confuse their targeted adults. Dr. Dan, who was so highly regarded in the community, and who used his medical training to mask much of his misconduct, also lied in a number of other ways that ensured his control of many situations. For instance, one neighbor remarked feeling uncomfortable one day when:

> Dr. Dan walked in without knocking. Suddenly I looked up from the kitchen table where I was having a morning cup of coffee, and there he was. I was flabbergasted. I didn't know what to say or do. He said, "Good morning. The door was open, so I thought I'd just pop in and see how Jimmy was doing. He seemed to have a bit of a cough at practice yesterday, and I just wanted to make sure he wasn't coming down with anything. Is he here?"

Jimmy had been up during the night with this cough, and his mother had been thinking of taking him to the doctor, although Dr. Dan was not the family doctor. She could hardly challenge his assertion that the door had been open, when first of all she could not be sure that one of the other kids had not left it ajar, and here was Dr. Dan being so helpful and attentive to her son, being willing to make a house call and save her time and money because now she would no longer need to take him to the doctor. Thus, she overlooked his assertion about the door being open, assumed that it must have been so, thereby ignoring her instinctual discomfort about having him just appear in her kitchen. Instead, she graciously accepted his assistance, thereby putting her son at risk (de Becker, 1999).

Once she allowed him to do this favor for her and her child, Dr. Dan had effectively used the lie to both get his foot in the door and put her in his debt, thereby creating some cognitive dissonance (Festinger, 1957) as she explained away her initial worries. Once in that position, and having accepted his help, it would become even less likely that she would in the future be clearer in recognizing his lies and stop him from blurring boundaries. When she was later describing the event to her friend, she had already altered her position to one of gratitude for Dr. Dan's help. Dr. Dan had prescribed codeine cough syrup for Jimmy, who had no further difficulty sleeping. The successful transition was not lost on Dr. Dan, who had carefully orchestrated the entire transaction.

The transaction also succeeded in communicating to Dr. Dan that this particular mother would easily allow boundaries to be blurred, and because she was now in his debt, it would become increasingly more difficult for her to stop him. Dr. Dan learned, "I can get away with this." For most people it would have taken much more assertiveness (and apparent rudeness to such a helpful neighbor) to confront such a seemingly minor lie, a challenge most people would be unable to manage. To Jimmy, Dr. Dan was now a welcome insider, because only extremely close and trusted friends and family had such easy access to the home.

Some of the lies told by child molesters are much more blatant, but equally effective. When the police were called to a party at Marvelous Marvin's house, they immediately focused on the alcohol being served to minors. Marvin, by graciously acknowledging this "error in judgment," and readily admitting to having a drinking problem, helped to distract them from paying attention to other more worrisome events. In this case, for instance, Marvin recalled that when the police arrived "one of the girls was undressed." Although the police did inquire about this, Marvin relied on his skills at lying, telling them, "She was trying to put on her bathing suit and needed me to help her with the straps." This was clearly a lie, and in fact he was already having sexual intercourse with this victim.

Because the best defense is a good offense, however, he exhibited a perfect blend of righteous indignation in combination with humility and embarrassment, telling the police, "If you don't believe me go ask her," thereby making himself appear to be perfectly comfortable in having them talk to the girl, while at the same time exhibiting remorse for the situation, noting, "I guess I have a drinking problem. That's probably why my judgment was poor. I should have let one of the other girls help her with the swim suit." Thus, he had admitted to a minor error in judgment and skillfully redirected the attention to that problem, thereby successfully taking charge of the ensuing investigation. In that context the officers felt no need to actually talk to the girl, something they would have experienced as awkward and uncomfortable. Marvin was quick to admit to the poor judgment, and the officers were impressed with his sincerity and remorse.

PHONY REMORSE

Child molesters can easily deliver alligator tears and remorse. Often, upon closer questioning, they are really only remorseful that they were caught, or sorry to be in the predicament, rather than what others presume they mean, which is regret for the harm they have caused to others. In fact, because the visible social skills are assumed by most people to reflect shared values, any expressed remorse and tears are interpreted as regret for the harm caused. In the case of child molesters, however, only very close scrutiny and a willingness to remain quiet or ask pointed questions will reveal that their words reflect a different experience.

When Marvelous Marvin delivered his "academy-award-winning performance" to avoid being convicted on the other counts of sexual misconduct, he referred to his sincere regrets about the events that had occurred. "I am so sorry about what happened. I can't believe the pain I've caused." People accepted his words at face value, but the pain he was referring to was his own pain, and he meant, "Of course I am remorseful. This has destroyed my marriage. My career is in a shambles. It's costing me a fortune in legal fees and therapy. This has ruined my life." This was not what people assumed he meant when he regretted his actions.

However, only by listening very carefully, without imposing assumed meanings onto the language used by the offender, can the true intentions be accurately heard. In extensive clinical evaluations, or during criminal investigations, this can be done only by taking careful notes, listening to the words, relying on clarification, and not engaging in the usual social interactions that occur between people who are in relationship. Friends and family who have reason to be somewhat suspicious or concerned about a potential child molester's intentions need to use the same skills in attending to the content rather than being swayed by assumptions made regarding the meaning of an offender's responses based on their performance or delivery.

CREATING RELATIONSHIP

Offenders very efficiently and successfully change the interactions with investigators or evaluators by establishing a collegial relationship. Since most people are raised to politely answer questions, some people even find themselves revealing personal material they would not normally freely disclose. Thus, during the first days of Businessman Bob's courtship with the woman who became his second wife, he asked her if she had ever been sexually abused as a child. She had never even talked to anybody about this before, and initially was somewhat taken aback, but after telling him about her past she very quickly felt much closer to him. The very process of responding to questions creates an alliance, however false. Answering personal questions instantly makes one feel much closer to the other person, a strategy child molesters use to their advantage.

Even during an investigation, child molesters may be quick to initiate a discussion with the investigator regarding how investigations are conducted, what can be learned by the questioning, or even initiating a conversation on the investigator's personal theories or experiences in the field. Once any such discussion is begun, the relationship between the one doing the investigation and the one being investigated has forever changed.

When police were called to question Marvelous Marvin about his having reportedly had sexual contact with a young boy, the investigating officer was relieved at the ease of what he expected would be a difficult task. Marvin quickly engaged him in conversation, commiserating with him, "This must be really hard for you to do." As a result, because the officer agreed with the challenge, finding the task rather embarrassing, the two of them became allies. The remainder of the investigation was simply a friendly chat, with the officer subsequently being assured that "nothing happened," it was "all a misunderstanding," and convinced the parents were "making a mountain out of a molehill."

INCONSISTENCIES

As already noted, child molesters lie about many things. Maintaining various lies becomes increasingly difficult, because if information provided about one event was fabricated, then giving further details about the event at some later date will invariably reveal inconsistencies. Attending to such inconsistencies is crucial in better understanding events. For instance, when Wanda first met Businessman Bob she knew there had been other girlfriends, and because she was hoping to establish a meaningful relationship, she was very curious about why each of these earlier relationships deteriorated. Bob told her that he had been together with one girlfriend for three years before "we called it quits. She needed a lot more attention than I could give her." When Wanda asked for more information, Bob elaborated, "The job I had at that time always had me out of town for three to four months at a time. She couldn't stand being alone. She found someone else who was around more." Partly because Wanda was also wondering whether Bob would leave her at some later date, she found this explanation reassuring, as she knew she would not be the one to leave.

However, at another time during his courtship with Wanda, Bob boasted about having earned his master's degree in business administration. He was quite proud of having managed to attend classes at night while working full time as well. Wanda could not bring herself to ask him how this was possible, as this story referred to the same time period when he was usually out of town for four months at a time, which had caused the girlfriend to leave him. She could not understand how Bob could have attended classes and maintained his grade point average when out of town so often. At first, she assumed she had misunderstood, and she said nothing. When it came up again later she actually asked him about it, but "He got so mad at me I figured it just wasn't worth it. I let it go. I did wonder about it, though. Later, when this all came out, I realized that things like that happened all the time."

Such inconsistencies often happen when talking to someone leading the double life that child molesters lead. However, the lies often also occur in the context of the offender brilliantly anticipating what the other person *wants* to hear. In fact, listeners who are either not "charmed" enough to ignore the inconsistencies, or intimidated enough to let it slide, would not be viewed as good targets and would therefore be less likely to have a child molester grooming them to gain access to children.

REHEARSED SPEECH

For people who tell lies, one way to avoid inconsistencies is to practice their stories in advance. However, the result is that the stories about prior events are always exactly the same. This would not be expected about important events that actually occurred, as each telling of the story should include variations in details and depth. Though actual facts about the event would remain the same, the storyteller would be expected to provide various embellishments with each telling. Child molesters often avoid the challenges of being caught lying by having carefully rehearsed, set speeches, providing the same descriptions each time.

Marvelous Marvin's first wife remembered that he was a great storyteller, always recounting funny incidents from his early years, but Marvin never really knew what information to include and what to omit. Thus, he rehearsed a number of set stories, then would test them on his wife. If she found them humorous, he would keep the "material." His wife thought knowing her husband's stories was just one of the prices couples paid for being in long-term, stable marriages. Whenever he went into one of the rehearsed stories, she would start attending to the needs of their visitors.

Evaluators interviewing identified child molesters often notice that the explanations they provide are verbatim of what they had previously told another investigator. In some cases, when extensive reports and transcripts exist, the person will provide a word-for-word account of events quoted in the transcripts ten years earlier.

TOO MUCH INFORMATION

Another technique often used by offenders is to provide greater detail than warranted given the situation, thereby creating the impression of someone who "doth protest too much." This actually distracts the listener, who becomes bogged down in irrelevant details and immaterial discrepancies, and is thereby sidetracked from the original topic.

Dr. Dan's wife began hearing some of the stories from the other mothers regarding her husband's somewhat "unorthodox" medical practices. When she confronted him about providing medical examinations to the boys on his team, wondering whether this was professionally suspect, he began a long, detailed, technical account of best medical practices, going off on tangents about possible sports injuries and case histories in which innocent coaches were sued for having ignored a player's sports injury. He interspersed his diatribe with comments such as: "I can't expect you to understand these matters since you haven't been to medical school." Soon his wife was busy refuting his accusations about her inability to understand the medical jargon, telling him, "I'm not stupid, you know." By the time the conversation came grinding to a halt, the initial question had been successfully buried.

GOING ON THE OFFENSIVE

As mentioned earlier, the best defense is a good offense, which the child molesters under discussion use to good effect. This technique quickly turns the tables, and the other person becomes defensive, feeling he or she must have made a mistake, thus terminating any further inquiry. This happened immediately when parents, after much trepidation, decided to talk to Cranky Coach Carl to ask him to stop touching the kids. He became furious:

> I can't believe this. You must have your mind in the gutter if that is what you think. I've been giving your boys all my attention to turn them into decent soccer players, and this is the thanks I get. I won't stand for this rudeness. If you don't want to talk to my lawyers you better stop this nonsense and apologize right now. I have never been so insulted in my life.

The parents, who had expected only to have the coach stop slapping their sons on the bottom and pulling down the children's pants, felt anxious and intimidated. The boys were uncomfortable with any such confrontation with the coach because it would guarantee that they would be both teased and benched. Therefore, nothing further was done by these parents.

Chapter 9

Predicting Risk

Child molesters live in the community. They are sons and daughters of community members, relatives, parents, grandparents, and neighbors. They have friends who admire them, and are often respected employees or bosses. Even after they have been convicted for committing a sexual assault against a child, even after they have completed SSOSA treatment, even after they have served time in prison, they return to the community. Even those who are civilly committed eventually are expected to return to the community. When child molesters return back to the community, family, friends, neighbors, and employers need to know how to welcome them back into the community without endangering children. In other words, communities need to learn to be "vigilant without becoming vigilante" (Halliday-Sumner, 1997), which requires community education and successful collaboration.

The community cannot afford the naïveté of Businessman Bob's new wife who thought he was safe because "he is a recovered child molester. He told me all about what he did, and he's been in therapy. I know I can trust him." Nor can the community tolerate judges who give custody to child molesters, as also happened to Bob because the judge reasoned, "the girls can put locks on their bedroom doors. That will provide ample protection from harm." Nor should the community endure a convicted child molester becoming a ski instructor who takes long leisurely hot-tub soaks with his young students, as Marvelous Marvin enjoyed because no one knew about his past.

Information about known child molesters should be properly understood and available on a national if not international database so that the offenders who frequently relocate can still be identifiable. Currently, little of this information is available. Those offenders who move easily escape detection because records are lost or misplaced, they change their name, or never appear on anyone's radar screen.

Bottom-feeder Buddy easily moved from town to town without ever having his prior convictions interfere with his ability to gain access to women who were happy to take him to homes where children lived.

COMMUNITY NOTIFICATION

Risk assessment strategies are used to attempt to differentiate the risk each convicted child molester poses to the community. This is intended to warn community members regarding those offenders who are released from prison, as well as to facilitate civil commitment procedures for those determined to present the greatest danger to the community. For those offenders who are viewed as dangerous but returned to the community, pictures and flyers are sent to warn community members. In Washington State, released child molesters are identified as being either Level I (low risk), Level II (intermediate risk), or Level III (high risk) child molesters. This assignment of risk, which also determines supervision requirements, is also based on the offender's conviction history. Thus, currently used risk determinations rely on the tip-of-the-iceberg information, namely the conviction record.

Level I offenders do not require community notification, but are obligated to register with local authorities so that the authorities know where they live. They are viewed as a low risk to the community because the offense was "nonviolent," and occurred in a family setting. Businessman Bob would be a Level I child molester, or "low risk," and therefore would not be viewed as being dangerous, which ignores much about his behavior that was never officially identified, including the earlier peeping, the sexual assault he committed in high school, and the children of prior girlfriends he molested. His second marriage provides him with renewed access to girls, as he busily grooms his stepdaughters, their friends, and his own daughters. Predictable Peter would also be viewed as a Level I child molester, which ignores a lifetime of continuous sexual assaults against all daughters and their girlfriends.

Level II child molesters require community notification. They are seen as being an intermediate risk because they had multiple offenses, and/or these occurred outside the family, or were seen as violent. The release of these offenders includes a flyer sent to neighbors and nearby schools describing the offense, a picture, and the offender's address, with required reporting by the offender of any address changes. Innocent Isaac had sex with a non-family member, his girlfriend Sally. He would be a Level II child molester, and would therefore be viewed as more dangerous than Businessman Bob or Predictable Peter upon his return to the community. Marvelous Moving Marvin, who was finally convicted for raping one girl, would possibly be rated as a Level II child molester because the girl was not a family member. Marvin, however, after successfully completing treatment, left the state, experiencing no further difficulties from the authorities.

Level III child molesters are seen as the most dangerous. Typically, these offenders are much more likely to be Grabbers rather than Groomers. They have more than one conviction, and their sexual offenses are officially identified as being predatory. Their return to the community includes a press release, in addition to the flyers sent to neighbors and nearby schools. Their pictures are published in the paper, and can be seen on Web sites run by local authorities. Most of the child molesters described in this book would never be identified as Level III offenders. Bottom-feeder Buddy, with a number of convictions, would be the most likely to eventually be viewed as a Level III child molester. Because he has no identifiable employment history, continuously moves, uses cash, and relies on the largesse of vulnerable women, he evaporates off any radar screen and is never seen again. As a result, he has continued easy access to children with reasonable impunity.

The community believes these Level III child molesters to be the most dangerous predators based on the numerical assignment of highest risk. Unfortunately, the more socially skilled Groomers described in this book are rarely identified as being Level III offenders despite their extensive sexually abusive activities. Although those assigned the status of Level III are, in fact, dangerous, the numerical assessment may generate a false sense of complacency regarding the danger posed by those offenders with lower risk labels. Developing numerical danger ratings was based on actuarial data, a statistical approach that may mask the danger Groomers present to the community.

WHAT IS ACTUARIAL DATA?

The topic of child sexual abuse is emotionally loaded, with most people having strong opinions about child molesters, variously sure the charges are "trumped up" against innocent men, or certain every offender is equally dangerous, or convinced a known offender would "never do this to my children." Emotional reactivity is not helpful in trying to understand the potential future risk each offender might present. Ideally, future danger could be calculated, thereby generating more focused supervision planning, as well as identifying management considerations for appropriate interventions to prevent further sexual assaults. In fact, if such information were accurate, intervention efforts could be focused on the most dangerous individuals, rather than worrying about offenders least likely to offend again.

Researchers working in this field recommend relying on actuarial approaches as the most accurate and scientific method for predicting the likelihood any given child molester will commit further offenses. Actuarial science is a statistical method for assigning numerical risk to studied behaviors by comparing one individual to similar, more extensively studied people and/or situations.

Actuarial data can be extremely helpful. For instance, the insurance industry relies on such statistical information to set coverage prices. Insurance companies know teenage boys have the highest accident rates, and therefore require them to pay more for car insurance. Although any one particular male teenager might be a safe driver, being a member of that group suggests a statistically greater likelihood of having a car accident. Elaborate statistical analyses can further show that young males who are good students and get higher grades are less risky and therefore some insurance companies provide discounts for good grades. Similar strategies establish health care premiums or life insurance rates. These techniques have been an effective and scientific way to assess individual risks of any studied group.

Using such an actuarial approach, for example, avoids mistaking an especially handsome young boy to be a safer driver just because "he sounds so sincere." The simple facts, in this case based on age, sex, and grades, provide tables indicating the likelihood of any given male having an accident. Statistical analyses could also suggest additional information to further mitigate his risk, such as driver's education.

A similar approach has been established for developing a clearer understanding of recidivism rates of convicted child molesters by incorporating the risk factors noted by researchers to be more highly correlated with further offending. Some of these approaches will be more closely examined.

Although actuarial data is helpful to insurance companies in setting insurance rates, it is currently insufficient for establishing risk among the grooming child molesters. This is because the actuarial statistics available to the insurance companies planning accident risk rates include all the data samples. Every traffic accident and/or fatality is recorded with relevant information about the driver made available. The same cannot be said, however, if one uses sexual abuse conviction data to represent the likelihood of future occurrences of sexual abuse when applying these practices to the well-socialized grooming child molesters. In their case, most of the relevant evidence is never incorporated into the data pool.

Actuarial versus Clinical Data

Researchers consider actuarial data a better predictor of future risk than clinical data. Clinicians could be easily fooled by the lies child molesters tell. After all, clinicians or therapists are trained to work on behalf of the client, and therefore are practiced at believing the information provided by the client, a distinction typically made between clinical and forensic psychological practices. Since voluntary clients seek therapy to improve interpersonal skills, lower stress, or change family dynamics, these clients are viewed as being reliable informants because they want help.

Groomer child molesters, however, are excellent liars who would easily misrepresent themselves to a clinician, and many of them are not necessarily interested in stopping the addiction. Their involvement in therapy is typically court ordered, and often serves the purpose of avoiding incarceration. They are not voluntarily seeking help, but hoping to avoid detection or minimize culpability. Furthermore, true disclosures regarding past conduct could result in more legal repercussions, further ensuring that offenders in treatment would be unlikely to voluntarily reveal everything. The clinical skills that therapists use to help voluntary clients do not work when evaluating child molester risk.

Research corroborates that actuarial approaches are superior in predicting future risk than can be expected from any clinical interview. The research comparing prediction efficacy between actuarial and clinical data understandably found clinical information to be less reliable, but also did not rely on entirely comparable studies (Litwack,

2001). For instance, some of the incorporated comparison clinical studies were intended for other purposes, such as predicting the suicide risk of psychiatric patients while in a hospital, rather than sexual recidivism risk of child molesters in the community, thus making the comparisons less than ideal. Other studies compared superficial clinical evaluations that were only intended to evaluate medication needs of patients while in a psychiatric hospital to more thorough actuarial approaches focused on assessing child molester risk, again minimizing the usefulness of comparisons.

DEFINING RECIDIVISM

Understanding the language used is also important. Various child molester risk assessments refer to "recidivism" rates. When relying on actuarial data to predict recidivism risk one might reasonably expect this to mean the likelihood that any given offender will molest again. However, this is misleading. The actuarial scales currently used were normed on criteria found to correlate with identified, convicted child molesters, whose subsequent sexual misconduct led to another arrest or another conviction (Doren, 2002) as a way to measure continued risk. In other words, the actuarial data provide statistical formulas for indicating the likelihood any given child molester has of being convicted for further sex offenses within a given time period when compared to the sample group(s).

The use of the word *recidivism* by experts is different than the use the public expects when hearing an offender described as being at "low risk to reoffend." The actuarial data cannot ascertain the likelihood of the person committing another sexual crime, but rather the likelihood of again being arrested and/or convicted for committing such a crime. The distinction between future risk of crime and future risk of arrest or conviction is profoundly important to the hundreds of children potentially molested by any given convicted child molester returning to the community.

It would be important to know how closely reconviction data parallel further actual sexual misconduct. If there were a direct correlation between sexual assaults and arrests and convictions, then relying only on such actuarial tools would be appropriate. The existence of such a direct correlation may be what distinguishes the Groomers from the Grabbers. Current actuarial scales may significantly underestimate the danger presented by the well-socialized child molesters described in this book whose misconduct rarely ever comes to the attention of the criminal justice system. Rather, the actuarial scales were normed on populations that may more closely resemble Grabbers, who are much more likely to be caught for a higher percentage of the actual crimes they commit. This would be expected for a number of reasons:

- *Grabbers attack strangers:* Victims are less likely to report sexual assaults by the Groomers because of all the reasons already described in this book: the assailant was a loved relative, friend, or respected authority figure, etc. No such alliance exists with attacks that are made by strangers.
- *The Grabber assault is clearer:* Sexual assaults by strangers are clearly attacks. Children are quicker to tell, they are more likely to be believed, there is less stigma against reporting, as well as clearer community support for such victims. Groomers create greater ambiguity using the adult support to prevent disclosures.
- *Grabber convictions are more likely:* Communities already have good methods in place when strangers are identified as sexually assaulting children. Since such assaults often occur in public places, there are also more witnesses available to help identify the assailant and ensure convictions.

The actuarial practices currently used provide statistical data useful in assessing risk on the Grabber population, but may miss much of the danger presented by the Groomers described in this book. Defining recidivism risk through conviction data (the tip of the iceberg) significantly underrepresents the dangerous ongoing activities of the well-socialized Groomers (the base of the iceberg). Because Groomers are unlikely to be caught, and when caught are extremely unlikely to reveal the true extent of their activities, the number of sex offenses committed by them is unlikely to have any direct correlation to conviction rates.

Another way to examine this dilemma is to use drunk driving convictions as a measure of alcohol consumption. First of all, not every drunk driving incident results in an arrest. In fact, most DWI (driving while intoxicated) or DUI (driving under the influence) arrests significantly underrepresent the true incident rates, as people often drive drunk without being ticketed. DWI data could reflect ongoing alcohol consumption with the more chaotic population of alcoholics who continue to drink and drive. Thus, like the Grabbers whose identified sexual attacks are more meaningfully reflected by their arrest rate, these drinkers would be more clearly identifiable with their ongoing arrests as being indicative of future risk of drinking.

A number of people who choose to continue drinking but take better precautions to never drive and drink again would become invisible should DWIs be used to measure alcohol consumption. This population would more closely resemble the Groomers who would use that first conviction to better avoid future detection. In the case of drinking they would continue to drink but they would be sophisticated enough to stop driving when drinking. In their case no further DWIs would not reflect sobriety, but would reflect better precautions about drinking.

Similarly, in the case of the grooming child molester, child sexual abuse convictions do not represent the occurrence of the behavior. Using conviction data to assess continued future risk would be similar to relying on DWI data to determine whether someone is continuing to drink any amount of alcohol. Too many intervening variables exist to have the DWI data be predictive regarding the likelihood of any alcohol consumption at all, as not all instances of drunk driving lead to a DWI, nor does someone need to drive if they have consumed alcohol.

This parallels information known about many of the Groomers under study who described their first conviction for a sexual offense to be "a wake-up call." As a result, they became more sophisticated in avoiding detection but no less active in their sexual misconduct. Marvelous Marvin described that after he was finally convicted, "I realized I had to be more careful. The counseling taught me to be more together as a person." He would be like the drinker who stopped driving but continued drinking. In the population of Groomers, the correlation between the activities of sexual assaults against children would not parallel their conviction record as closely as would be expected of the Grabber population. This would indicate that relying on actuarial data alone could severely underestimate risk, but never overestimate danger.

BASE RATE

Researchers relying on actuarial data argue that the sexual assaults are rare. As a result, because the base rate of the event occurring, namely a sexual assault, is so low in the first place, the likelihood of another offense is extremely low. However, when one looks at the actual behavior of Groomers, the frequency of their misconduct is anything but low. Rather, Groomers are continuously busy with activities directed at having sexual contact with children. *Being convicted* for such offenses is what is low.

In fact, the most dramatic behavioral characteristic of the Groomers described in this book is the high frequency and intensity of offending. They do not coach only one soccer team; they coach five teams, and tutor dozens of children when they are not leading the youth group at church. There is no room in their life for anything but making a living, grooming parents and communities, and accessing children. Dr. Dan ran a boys club, coached baseball, and took children camping and skiing. Marvelous Marvin babysat, worked as a youth group leader, and was continuously around children. He admitted having sexually molested over 200 children by the time he was in his early twenties. Some of these children he touched briefly, many others were assaulted numerous times, with the sexualized touching increasing in intensity as he groomed them into the "relationship." Even Coach Carl, when not out of town on sex trips, was constantly involved in soccer, coaching teams, running the league, and refereeing games—all opportunities to gain access to children and to mask his continued sexual misconduct. The base rate for these offenders was continuous. Other research tools will be required to more effectively identify the ongoing risk and to more meaningfully intervene when dealing with the Groomer child molesters.

DETERMINING RISK

Future research developing actuarial data on this population would need to incorporate community data. The grooming strategies, the innuendoes, and concerns by friends and neighbors, would all be crucial to understanding the frequency of the behavior and the likelihood it will continue. However, unlike the Grabbers, without meaningful intervention and monitoring these Groomers would correctly be viewed as extremely likely to continue to behave in the future exactly as they have behaved in the past. Intervention strategies would need to incorporate community awareness with the ongoing lifetime commitments to treatment required to successfully manage any addictive behavior.

The Groomers under study are extremely predictable, and because their activities and methods are not as invisible as had been previously thought, once they are unmasked, they can be prevented from having continued access to children through close community collaboration, in combination with careful ongoing supervision and monitoring.

CORROBORATING DATA

Neither current actuarial data nor clinical data suffice in identifying risk with the grooming child molester population. What is most needed is corroborating data. Current practices fail to include the information known by people who have been in direct relationship with the offender. Therefore, current investigations lack much of the relevant evidence needed to accurately differentiate dangerous offenders from the less harmful, and lack information crucial to making sufficiently meaningful supervision, treatment, and management recommendations. By ignoring this rich, community-based evidence, current practices often predict these well-socialized child molesters to be safer than would be accurate.

For instance, Marvelous Marvin, who continuously caused consternation to many of the people who encountered him, and whose behavior can most accurately be explained as nonstop, goal-directed activities toward accessing children and molesting children, is clearly different from Truthful Tim, the teacher who came to the attention of his employers because of a disgruntled colleague whose advances he rebuffed. Dr. Dan, Predictable Peter, Businessman Bob, and even Coach Carl have very different profiles from the profile revealed by examining Innocent Isaac's history.

Coach Carl has never been convicted of a sexual assault, nor has Dr. Dan, while Businessman Bob, Marvelous Moving Marvin, and Predictable Peter each have only one sexually related conviction. Therefore, were one to rely on conviction data only, one would incorrectly assume Coach Carl and Dr. Dan to be less dangerous than Innocent Isaac with one conviction. In fact, Innocent Isaac would incorrectly be viewed as being equally dangerous as Predictable Peter, Businessman Bob, or Marvelous Marvin, who all also have one conviction each. Viewing them as being equally risky to the community ignores the fact that the latter three are clearly dangerous to children while Innocent Isaac is not.

Society cannot afford these errors in predicting risk, both because the reputations and lives of innocent people are unnecessarily ruined, and because those who are truly dangerous all too often disappear beneath the radar screen. In fact, Marvelous Marvin, with only one conviction, left the community to lead a much more transient life, thereby further lowering the risk of detection. In each new community where he lives, those who eventually begin to worry about his conduct and to question his practices are relieved when he disappears. This allows them to do nothing. Complaints made to employers in every new community disappear as well. Whenever employers are later asked to provide a reference, they never mention anything about these concerns because of worries about legal repercussions. As a result, only glowing references follow him to every new town, with each past employer glad to escape a sticky dilemma.

The problem is, of course, that in most cases, the available clues that eventually lead individuals to become concerned that a person might be a child molester never become known to anyone else, and never become officially identified. Such suppression of relevant information masks the very evidence needed to more accurately differentiate those people who are the most dangerous from those who present a lower risk. Not including such vital information ensures that those deemed to be dangerous, based on conviction data, are truly extremely dangerous. Therefore, community notifications identifying a child molester returning to the community as a Level III offender can only understate the danger rather than exaggerate the risk. Rather, by ignoring the community-based evidence, some very dangerous offenders could seem harmless. Ignoring such data would suggest Businessman Bob to be benign, only a one-time "incest" offender. Relying only on conviction data would even make some innocent people appear more dangerous while allowing some of the truly dangerous to escape further detection.

THE PROBLEM WITH NUMBERS

Child molesters present an ongoing danger to the community, and this danger continues despite attempts at intervention, treatment, and/or incarceration (Schlank & Cohen, 1999). Risk assessments are done precisely to better establish the danger that a known child molester would present to the community upon release. In some states and in Canada, civil commitment is also considered for child molesters viewed as too dangerous (predatory) to return to the community even after serving a prison sentence.

The desire to more accurately differentiate those who will commit further sex offenses from those who will not is a complicated process (Doren, 1998; Hanson, 1998). Incorrectly deeming someone as a continued, clear danger to the community, as would be true if one considered either Truthful Tim or Innocent Isaac to be dangerous, would erode principals of individual liberties that are held dear to democratic societies. Failing to identify someone as dangerous, as would be the case should Marvelous Marvin, Predictable Peter, Businessman Bob, Divine Dr. Dan, or Coach Carl's conduct be ignored, inappropriately endangers the public. Mistakenly releasing child molesters who subsequently commit more heinous crimes, results in bad press for the professionals involved, and wrongful harm lawsuits for the institutions. Worst of all, however, such errors ensure continued danger to children, as evidenced by both Businessman Bob and Marvelous Marvin's ongoing conduct after their convictions. However, restricting someone unnecessarily robs them of their civil rights.

The more accurately future risk can be understood and predicted, the better. Unfortunately, feedback regarding the accuracy of past predictions is scarce, as those predicting the future do not have adequate, subsequent, community-based data. Offenders who remain incarcerated protest that they were falsely judged, that the past was wrongly held against them, or argue they could safely be released, insisting:

> "I've learned my lesson."
> "I would never do this again."
> "I will stop drinking and that will solve the problem."

Determining recidivism by asking them about earlier misconduct is also unreliable as most child molesters would be very unlikely to reveal anything about their prior behavior that was not already on the official record. Child molesters in prison treatment programs also know better than to disclose everything, because disclosures about behavior not previously identified could result in further convictions.

Applying actuarial scales to ascertain risk results in a numerical determination regarding the potential for future danger. Although researchers and specialists understand this in the correct context, once numbers are assigned, the numbers create their own reality. The public is used to hearing numbers and applying them to daily decision making. For instance, learning it will be 80 degrees Fahrenheit with low humidity is meaningfully different from below-freezing weather. Sailors hearing about gale warnings know to stay home, and skiers informed about twenty inches of new powder and clear skies know to go skiing. Assessing child molester dangerousness with numbers and numerical ratings (low, medium, high), or the percentages assigned by the different actuarial scales implies scientific accuracy that may be misleading. When the public learns a released child molester has a lower than 10 percent likelihood of recidivism within a six-year period they assume the rating to be meaningful.

Assessing risk by using the currently available actuarial approaches should be more closely examined. The actuarial data are based only on information available at the tip of the iceberg, rather than qualitative, available information. Since the Groomer cases represent a significant percentage of the danger to children caused by child molesters, limitations to the actuarial approach cannot be ignored because a number of truly dangerous individuals will incorrectly appear harmless. Suggesting that such errors are infrequent or minor would also be misleading. Errors in actuarial scales are errors in underreporting danger, never in overreporting danger.

Actuarial Scales

A number of risk assessment instruments have been developed for evaluating child molester danger. These include the Rapid Risk Assessment for Sexual Offense Recidivism (RRASOR; Hanson et al., 1997), Minnesota Sex Offender Screening Tool-Revised (MnSOST-R; Epperson, Kaul, & Huot, 1995), Psychopathy Checklist-Revised (PCL-R; Hare, 1991), Violence Risk Appraisal Guide (VRAG; Webster, Harris, Rice, Cormier, & Quinsey, 1994), and the Sex Offender Risk Appraisal Guide (SORAG; Quinsey, Harris, Rice, & Cormier, 1998). Although the VRAG and SORAG (Schlank & Cohen, 1999) are more sensitive to evaluating general criminal behavior, rather than specifically identifying continued risk for sexual recidivism, the instruments are included here because they are frequently used in risk assessments.

These instruments tap into a number of identified behaviors, which according to the research, are generally associated with increased risk (Hanson & Bussiere, 1998). By examining conviction records of varying groups of child molesters, the presumable likelihood that other similar populations would be convicted again for their sexual misconduct can be statistically identified.

The criteria used in the actuarial studies were based on agreed-upon risk factors noted as being predictors of risk among varying child molester populations. The cases discussed in this book will be examined in light of these criteria.

A Sexual Preference for Children

According to a number of researchers, phallometric data are a strong predictor of future risk for further sex offending (Quinsey, Lalumiere, Rice, & Harris, 1995; Schlank & Cohen, 2001). Plethysmograph data (a measurement of arousal through penile engorgement) was obtained on Businessman Bob while he was in SSOSA, revealing arousal to both adult females and even stronger arousal to girls and adolescent females. After Marvelous Marvin's rape conviction, plethysmograph data obtained during sex offender treatment revealed strongest arousal to young boys, followed by arousal to preteen girls. Only moderate arousal to adult females was noted, and there was no evidence of arousal to adult males. No plethysmograph data were ever obtained on Predictable Peter as he denied the offense and refused treatment, preferring to go to jail rather than admit guilt. Dr. Dan and Coach Carl were never convicted, so there were no plethysmograph data available on them. Innocent Isaac, who had been convicted and participated in SSOSA, was aroused only to peer-aged females.

Marvin continued to actively associate almost exclusively with children, only dating adult females who already had children. Dr. Dan remained married, but almost continuously surrounded himself with young boys. Businessman Bob married again, this time to a woman who already had young daughters. In fact, his second wife, who had been sexually abused as a child, and whose daughters had been molested by her first husband, considered Businessman Bob to be especially safe because he so openly admitted his past and had completed child molester treatment.

I figured he was perfect. He told me all about his treatment, and he was so open with me about having molested his daughter. He cried about how ashamed he was. He begged me to meet his therapist so that I would understand what he had gone through.

Although some pedophiles respond exclusively to children (APA, 2000), a number of practicing child molesters endorse experiencing sexual arousal to both adults and children (Silva, 1990; Cook, 1989), and many seemingly sexually appropriate and married individuals are also child molesters (van Dam, 1996, 2001). Other child molesters describe being sexual with adults by fantasizing the partner to be a child. Without closer inspection on a case-by-case basis, it is not possible to know when child molesters establish adult sexual relationships primarily to obtain access to children, or whether they experience sexual arousal to both adult and child stimuli. It is misleading, however, to assume the risk of continued sexual assaults to decrease because an offender has developed a sexual peer relationship.

Any Deviant Sexual Preference

Evidence of any other deviant sexual preference is also associated with increased risk. In the cases of Marvin, Dr. Dan, Businessman Bob, and Coach Carl, the very act of molesting children reflects sexually deviant behavior. Without closer clinical scrutiny it would be unknown whether this is a preferred sexual outlet. Some of the literature minimizes sexual deviance among married men, considering it as evidence of their wives' failure to be sexually responsive (Rush, 1980; Salter, 1995), thereby viewing the child molester as victim, rather than perpetrator. Understandably, molesters prefer this explanation, which incorrectly exonerates harmful and illegal behavior, inappropriately externalizes responsibility, and wrongly categorizes married molesters as being less predatory.

Predictable Peter remained happily married yet continuously molested female children. Marvin was sexually involved with adults, yet steadily molested children. This was also true for Dr. Dan, who maintained a seemingly normal marital relationship while seeking out boys to molest. Coach Carl had been married at one time, but never remarried. He focused entirely on adolescent boys, and when not molesting children he had groomed through his coaching, he took sexual excursions first to the Orient, and then later to Central America, where young "prostitutes" are a major industry, attracting vacation-ing pedophiles to a haven away from detection.

Prior Sexual Offenses

Since identified sexual offenses are generally agreed to represent only the tip of the iceberg (Greenberg, 1998), any prior sexual offense should be highly correlated with continued risk. In fact, in many ways, the best predictor of future behavior is past behavior (Monahan, 1981; Klassan & O'Connor, 1994), and a prior history of any sexual offense could suggest continued risk. However, many times the initial offense occurs only after an extensive history of sexual offending that never comes to the attention of the criminal justice system, as was the case with Predictable Peter, Marvelous Marvin, and Businessman Bob. As already noted, risk assessment instruments primarily rely on conviction data to establish a record of past behavior. As a result, the risk assessment scales would suggest that Innocent Isaac, convicted for having been sexual with his girlfriend, would present the same fu-ture risk as Predictable Peter, Marvelous Marvin, or Businessman Bob, yet the latter three are clearly more dangerous to children. Further-more, because evidence of this behavior so rarely surfaces (Brongersma, 1991; Abel, Becker, Mittleman, Rouleau, & Murphy, 1987), convic-tions for such individuals as Marvelous Marvin, Predictable Peter, and Businessman Bob should be viewed as highly significant. The additional charges against Marvelous Marvin, in combination with recurring indications from both children and adults reporting prior abuse, should all be considered as suggesting the likelihood of signif-icantly more sexual abuse activity than officially identified.

Failure to Complete Treatment

Failure to complete child molester treatment has been associated with increased future risk (Looman, Abracen, & Nicholaichuk, 2000), although this does not mean that treatment completion can be associ-ated with decreased risk (Barbaree, 1997; Marques, Day, Nelson, & West, 1994). Treatment efficacy remains controversial (Marshall & Pithers, 1994; Alexander, 1999), and a number of studies suggest that those who successfully complete treatment may be learning to better evade future detection, rather than controlling sexual deviancy (Seto & Barbaree, 1999). Businessman Bob used the treatment to his advantage by convincing his second wife that he was now recovered. Marvelous Marvin found the therapy to be useful in learning to better mask his behavior, and developing improved radar to sense when his misconduct made it necessary to leave town. Innocent Isaac found treatment uncomfortable. He had never before thought about sex with children. Treatment had no impact on Businessman Bob's subsequent behavior. In fact, he enjoyed treatment because "I learned a lot about ways to access children I didn't already know," which revealed his failure to internalize the cognitive shifts typically taught in sex offender treatment programs.

Antisocial Personality Disorder and Psychopathy

Criminal versatility and psychopathic tendencies are associated with an increased risk of continued offending. In fact, "antisocial child molesters are much more likely to recidivate with a nonsexual crime than with a sexual crime" (Hanson, in Schlank & Cohen, 1999, pp. 8-18). But, unlike the child molester who engages in a number of other antisocial behaviors, only Bottom-Feeder Buddy had committed any other crimes. None of the other offenders described in this book had any other criminal history. This is true for many of the successfully socialized child molesters, thereby suggesting that only the least effective child molesters, and/or the Grabbers, ever even come to the attention of the criminal justice system for other types of misconduct. As a result, the successful child molesters described in this book would obtain lower scores on the Psychopathy Checklist-Revised (Hare, 1991), with any assigned score only reflecting the narcissistic tendencies commonly noted among this population.

Any Prior Offenses

Continued risk for further sexual offenses is commonly viewed as more likely among those with a criminal history of sexual misconduct. As already stated, however, the sexual improprieties of the offenders described in this book did not result in earlier convictions. Reliance on such history would incorrectly make them appear less dangerous. Successful child molesters are often exemplary citizens accorded numerous accolades (van Dam, 2001). Using criminal versatility to gauge risk would help them escape detection. Father John Geoghan had never been charged or convicted for any of the hundreds of children he molested over more than twenty years (The Investigative Staff of *The Boston Globe*, 2002). The otherwise exemplary behavior falsely masks danger when only relying on prior offenses to evaluate risk.

Age

Increased age is generally correlated with decreased risk (Hanson & Bussiere, 1998; Quinsey et al., 1998; Schlank & Cohen, 1999). Though the research would suggest overtly visible antisocial behavior generally decreases after middle age (APA, 2000), there is no evidence to indicate that sexual misconduct parallels this pattern. Rather, child molesters describe becoming more adroit with age, with increasing respect further decreasing the likelihood of being accused. Marvelous Marvin became more sophisticated at evading detection. Businessman Bob used his standing in the community to mask continued sex-offending behavior. Predictable Peter only came to the attention of the criminal justice system at the age of seventy, despite a lifetime of sexual misconduct. His subsequent behavior in the hospital, when all social control was lost, revealed the underlying sexual addiction for all to see. Demented and delusional, he continuously tried to lure the nurses into his clutches with offers of candy, visibly reenacting techniques previously described by his young victims.

Never Married

The research suggests that those molesters who never married are at increased risk to reoffend (Hanson & Bussiere, 1998). Many of the more successful child molesters maintain steady adult sexual relationships. To suggest that marital status decreases the likelihood of sexual misconduct among this population would be wrong. Businessman Bob, Marvelous Marvin, Coach Carl, Predictable Peter, and Dr. Dan were all in varying sexual relationships with peers. In fact, Businessman Bob found marriages helped provide him with easier access to female children. Dr. Dan viewed the two lives he led as separate but parallel. He enjoyed a home, loved his daughter, but found the additional sexual activities with young boys to be much more exciting than anything he ever experienced with his wife. He also recognized maintaining his home environment improved his community standing, which further protected his addictive secret. A number of prolifically active child molesters, who appear socially appropriate, are married (van Dam, 1996). Innocent Isaac, who never was a child molester, would appear more dangerous because he is still single.

Any Unrelated Victims

In general, it is presumed that those who molest unrelated victims are at higher risk to reoffend, with the assumption that incest offenders are a different category of offender than those who sexually abuse other people's children. Dr. Dan certainly molested children outside his home, although had he had sons he may have molested them as well. Businessman Bob, however, molested his own daughter, as well as seeking girlfriends and wives with young girls in the home to provide ready access to his preferred victims. He also encouraged these girls to bring friends to the home, thereby providing him with access to more children to molest. Marvelous Marvin similarly molested children in the home as well as any other children he could access through work and play. There is insufficient research to confirm that all incest offenders are safer; anecdotal experience with thousands of socially skilled child molesters suggests otherwise.

Any Male Child Victims

The research suggests that those who molest males pose a greater danger as they are seen as being more likely to reoffend. This is because they often have higher numbers of known victims. Many of the assaults against males, however, include brief contacts, such as frottage, thereby resulting in some of these offenders having thousands of victims, although the harm to each victim would be less than in cases where the abuse was longer lasting and/or more invasive. Viewing these potentially briefer assaults as being more dangerous, and thereby identifying that those who molest male children are at greater risk to offend again is misleading.

This is insufficient as a criterion for differentiating between the two populations or to consider those who molest males as being more dangerous. Predictable Peter focused only on females, but molested all the female children in his social sphere. Dr. Dan, who focused only on males, had brief contact assaults with some of them and established closer and more enduring sexual interactions with a chosen few. Marvelous Marvin sexually assaulted both males and females.

Applying the Actuarial Data

Families who encounter child molesters obtain information rarely incorporated in actuarial data. Community members may slowly learn more and more about a child molester in their midst, and have relevant evidence that should be incorporated in understanding and predicting continued risk. Neither Coach Carl nor Dr. Dan was ever convicted. Actuarial scales could not be applied to them, and they would be viewed as presenting no risk to the public. This would, however, ignore their behavior. Similarly, Truthful Tim has never been convicted, and he would appear to present no risk, but large qualitative differences exist between Coach Carl's and Dr. Dan's behavior versus Truthful Tim's conduct that should not be ignored when addressing public safety. Similarly, by relying on conviction data, Innocent Isaac, Marvelous Marvin, Predictable Peter, and Businessman Bob would all appear to be equally dangerous. This again ignores the rich qualitative evidence that reveals large discrepancies between Innocent Isaac's behavior and the others, discrepancies that should be viewed as very relevant when looking at public safety.

RRASOR

RRASOR examines risk by assigning points based on the following items:

1. Prior sex offense conviction(s)
2. Over age twenty-five on release
3. Any male victims
4. Any nonrelated victims

This instrument cannot be used without one prior conviction for a sexual offense. Thus, this would not apply to Coach Carl or Dr. Dan who have no convictions.

Predictable Peter had no prior convictions for sexual misconduct, was over age twenty-five, had no convictions for molesting males, and being convicted for having molested a family member, namely his granddaughter, would obtain a score of 0. Thus, based on a comparison group of approximately 527 studied offenders, he would be viewed as being at the lowest risk possible for committing any further sexual crimes, which would be viewed as less than anywhere between 4.4 percent to 6.5 percent within a five-to-ten-year follow-up period.

Businessman Bob, similarly would obtain a score of 0, and would be viewed in the lowest possible risk range, having no prior sex offenses, being over twenty-five, and being convicted for molesting a related female.

Innocent Isaac, on the other hand, would look significantly more sinister. He had no prior sex offenses, but is less than twenty-five years old, and molested an unrelated female. Thus, he would be assigned a score of 2, which when compared with a sample population of 742 child molesters, would predict anywhere from a 14.2 to 21.1 percent recidivism risk within a five-to-ten-year period.

Marvelous Marvin would look no different from Innocent Isaac, also being assigned a score of 2 in the same categories.

MnSOST-R

The historical data were also used to provide an MnSOST-R score subsequent to each of the convictions/incarcerations. This scale was not normed on incest offenders. Thus, it could not be applied for evaluating risk on Businessman Bob or Predictable Peter as their convictions were incestuous. This scale incorporates more background information, thus individuals who have also committed other crimes or those with extensive histories of unemployment and chemical dependency obtain higher scores. On this scale, however, the current sexual crime is included in determining risk. None of the other cases used during this evaluation would appear particularly worrisome on this scale. Marvelous Marvin obtained a score of -10; Innocent Issac obtained a higher score of -8 because the sexual intercourse took place outdoors under the stars. His apparent risk increased as per test criteria. Neither of these scores, however, would correspond to high future risk, with both of them below the lowest risk range in the normative samples. As a result, both would be viewed as extremely unlikely to commit any further sex offenses within the next six-year period. Although this correctly applies to Innocent Isaac, it masks the danger that Marvelous Marvin presents.

Psychopathy (PCL-R)

The Hare Psychopathy Checklist requires extensive clinical judgment in assigning scores, and is best done only when there is significant, extensive, corroborating information. Most of the individuals examined in this book have led law-abiding, steady lives, have not frequently changed marital partners (although Marvelous Marvin began doing so after leaving town), have no childhood history of juvenile misconduct, and have no other overtly identifiable features consistent with psychopathy. Though they lack empathy, and experience no real remorse, as known by their actual behaviors, this could not be ascertained by the available information. Bottom-feeder Buddy, on the other hand, should he ever surface long enough to be accurately assessed, would be seen as evidencing greater psychopathy than the other Groomers described in this book.

SORAG

This instrument was designed (Quinsey et al., 1998) to look more specifically at the risk presented by child molesters, and more accurately addresses the risk of further violence per se. It includes PCL-R data in assessing risk scores. All four of the cases under study would have been viewed as low risk. Predictable Peter, with his advanced age, long marriage, and stable life history, would score the lowest of the group at -19, which would correspond to anywhere from an 8 to 10 percent likelihood of further criminal conduct within the next seven-to-ten-year period. Businessman Bob, with a score of -15, would be viewed as having a similar future risk. Both Innocent Isaac and Marvelous Marvin would be seen as equally likely to reoffend within the next seven to ten years, with anywhere from a 12 to 24 percent recidivism risk.

Numbers Can be Misleading

Danger exists in assigning these numerical values. Numbers that view Innocent Isaac as being much more dangerous than either Businessman Bob or Predictable Peter, and consider his future risk as similar to Marvelous Marvin's, are especially problematic. Society assigns the same validity to these numbers as it does to the multitude of other numbers used on a daily basis. This is misleading information that serves the child molesters more than it serves the public.

Chapter 10

Incorporating Corroborating Evidence

Correctly differentiating between Groomers who molest children and individuals innocent of any sexual wrongdoing would not be as complex if those in charge of determining risk and danger had access to all the information. As already noted in the cases described in this book, there are large differences in the daily practices and habits of those who spend all their time focusing on accessing children to satiate their sexual desires, as opposed to those who are not so inclined.

Evaluating this danger cannot rely only on information provided by the offender. In fact, any information that relies on their reports can be presumed to include distortions, lies, minimizations of events, or misrepresentations of the truth. Unfortunately, those who deal with offenders professionally, namely the police, prosecutors, judges, juries, and professionals responsible for their treatment and follow-up management, can similarly be gullible to their lies. This is because, as a group, child molesters are among the most effective liars in the world.

Often, the information made available to the authorities includes earlier reports in which previous investigators or interviewers relied on information provided solely by the alleged offender. Once that information is incorporated in a report, it starts looking like third-party evidence, even though it was initially information reported only by the offender. The information then becomes established as fact, almost lending an official credence to that data, and sooner or later information initially made available by the offender can become part of the official record used in assessing risk. Since much of the information used in the actuarial tools relies on data often known only by the offender, this becomes part of the official record as well. For instance, infidelity during marriage, work history, and home life while growing up (incorporated risk assessments) are all details about the individual in which the truth may be at variance with what eventually is accepted as having occurred.

Assessing risk must include the information known about the individual by all those who have had concerns. Without such corroborating data, for instance, Marvelous Marvin, with his one conviction for sexually assaulting a girl, would not be properly viewed as a very effective and dangerous offender, while Innocent Isaac, because one sexual liaison occurred outside on a blanket under a starry summer sky, would be deemed more dangerous. The people who have dealt with child molesters, however, have access to rich information that would greatly help investigators and subsequent decision makers better understand the patterns of misconduct and the risks they present to children. Groomer child molesters continuously cause others to be concerned; their behavior is frequently viewed with raised eyebrows everywhere they go, and their activities are directed toward gaining access to children, unlike those who are innocent of such improprieties. However, because these child molesters go to such great lengths to appear above reproach, any superficial investigation regarding the opinions of those who do not know the alleged offender well could include only high praise.

For this reason many of the most notoriously active and successful child molesters, when finally identified through an official allegation to the police, receive glowing letters of support, as well as letters of shock and outrage that such a "fine upstanding" citizen would be so viciously maligned. These letters should be viewed in the context of possibly reflecting the image management Groomer child molesters do all too well. Instead, those who have had to live with the offender, neighbors, former colleagues, former girlfriends, as well as people who had contact with the offender when they were children, would all be in a better position to provide much richer information about the person's prior behavioral habits. Investigators need to talk to these individuals, and they need to ask the right questions to unearth information that would be useful in making a correct determination. Only through such an investigation would the information known at the base of the iceberg become visible to the investigators and evaluators.

It is important to remember Innocent Isaac's dilemma as well. His earnest protestations of innocence sound exactly like the pseudosincere lies of Groomer pedophiles. Only a thorough investigation of the cases would reveal the significant behavioral patterns, not visible through conviction records, necessary for differentiating the grooming sexual addict from the innocent.

Whereas the Grabbers may be playing by entirely different behavioral rules, the Groomers described in this book, and studied by the thousands, suffer from an addiction, with everything about their habits and practices being visible for those trained and/or willing to see. In the workplace, the Groomer is well liked and extremely helpful to others. He earns everyone's trust with selflessness and sincerity. If he serves on community boards it is to obtain respectability to gain access to parents with target-age children. If he goes to church he goes as a hunter or cunning predator. Social events are a high priority because of the opportunities to begin the parent-grooming process anew. Groomers are on active duty virtually every waking hour, which is precisely what is expected from an addict. Everyone they encounter is either part of the solution or of no further use. Most important of all is that they quickly disappear when not properly supported. Understanding this addictive quality, and recognizing the grooming behaviors are how they are unmasked.

The grooming child molesters whose overtures are not welcomed move on to another family, another town, and ultimately another state or province until they land successfully. Communities working together at all levels can intervene by not being charmed, reporting concerns, tracking the different complaints, and generally sending the message that the adults are collaborating to protect the children. This is done at every level.

Secrecy and isolation allows child sexual abuse to occur and to flourish. Secrecy and isolation protects the offenders. The antidote is open communication and networking. Neither the victims, nor the families of victims should be embarrassed, ashamed, or afraid of having been targeted by a child molester. They did nothing wrong. The child molesters are the ones who should be afraid. To date, these child molesters have retained the upper hand. They have kept their victims isolated and afraid, and used the shame and discomfort most people associate with sexual matters to wreak continued havoc on the community's children. This silence has provided them with a protective shield.

Much of the damage resulting from child sexual abuse is the victim's loss of power and control. Skilled therapists are aware that helping survivors regain power and control over their lives is crucial to recovery, while knowing not to create false memories in those who were never abused. Appropriate therapeutic efforts also entail giving community members the power and control to identify child molesters, convict child molesters, and then more meaningfully monitor child molesters when they return to the community to ensure that no more children be victimized.

The Groomers described in this book should be the ones to be ashamed and afraid. Many of them have left a trail of hundreds of witnesses whose information should correctly put the problem in the right perspective. Their victims, the parents of their victims, and all community members who wish to protect children from harm can together make the world less safe for child molesters.

In the early 1980s, Linda Halliday-Sumner created a movement in one small Canadian town. Her organization of Sexual Abuse Victims Anonymous (SAVA) provided a support network for victims. Through her efforts, victims participated in self-help activities that included actively pursuing legal action. As a result, the police and the courts in that community became increasingly skilled at knowing what to do. One judge remarked that he knew whenever he had a sexual assault trial because all the other SAVA members would be in the courtroom, supporting the victim, and ready to stage a press conference if the case were mishandled. As a result of Linda Halliday-Sumner's efforts during those years, the conviction rate for child sexual abuse skyrocketed. Whereas only one sexual abuse case was prosecuted during the previous eight-year period, in the following three-year period "35 offenders were charged in 36 cases," this because "one offender was tried twice on separate charges within two years" (van Dam, Halliday, & Bates, 1985, p. 108). These victims were empowered by their ability to come forward, be supported, and right the wrongs. SAVA proved the importance and effectiveness of networking and community collaboration.

VICTIMS

Victims are the most powerful resource for protecting children from known child molesters. Individuals who have been sexually molested are the best informants because they know what happened. They can name the molester and they can provide detailed information regarding the abuse. Furthermore, their information is not hearsay. Victims keep quiet for many different reasons, including fear,

Boys

shame, and embarrassment. Telling about abuse is frightening when they are children, and continues to be frightening and emotionally difficult even years later when they are adults. Too often, victims assume they were the only ones ever molested by the offender. They fail to understand how their information can protect others, and instead continue to keep the secret. This only serves to protect offenders.

In one small town, handsome, successful, thirty-five-year-old Jim had kept the secret about his abuse at the hands of his uncle. The events continued to haunt him, yet for twenty-five years he never told a soul. Local newspaper coverage of a prominent sexual abuse trial finally brought this man to therapy. Because of all the newspaper coverage detailing the sexual abuse of hundreds of young boys by one offender he realized his situation was not unique. From his therapist, he learned about the dynamics of child sexual abuse. Through treatment, he realized he had nothing to be ashamed of. When the therapist learned the uncle was a soccer coach who was still actively involved with children, Jim was encouraged to talk to the police.

Jim told police about the abuse by his uncle, Cranky Coach Carl, who now lived across the country but was actively coaching boys' soccer. The police contacted officials in Coach Carl's town, who began an investigation. Coach Carl's world finally collapsed as a number of boys described events that occurred in hotel rooms during out-of-town soccer games. The case went to trial where a group of frightened young boys testified. Jim recalled feeling like a conquering hero walking into the courtroom. "I told the judge and the jury 'He did this to me too.'" Coach Carl was finally convicted at age fifty-five for sexually molesting boys on his soccer team. Jim no longer felt like a victim. He no longer felt ashamed. He was proud of his contribution. He also felt that he was fortunate. His immediate family supported him although numerous aunts and uncles considered his actions hateful and despicable. Jim's therapist had adequately prepared him for all the challenges and the rewards he could expect in reporting his uncle to the police. Jim said,

> Doing this was the scariest thing I ever did in my whole life. It was also the most rewarding thing. I felt so good walking into that courtroom. I was the hero. It was my testimony that helped all those other kids. Since then my life has gotten so much better. I used to be afraid of relationships. I was never close to anyone before, I always wondered if maybe I was a homosexual because of what my uncle did. I never really dated.

Since then, Jim has returned to school, obtained a master's degree, and met the woman he subsequently married. "My uncle's family still won't talk to me. My mother says they won't talk to her either. But my mom and dad and I—we know we did the right thing."

Victims should report the abuse. However, they should never do this alone and in isolation because of the many complications that always arise. When highly regarded individuals are accused of child sexual abuse, friends and allies of the accused go on the attack, loyalties become divided, and victims too often find themselves victimized again. Sexual assault centers, with trained therapists, are ideally suited to help victims gain the courage to report, and the support to follow through in any subsequent legal case. Sexual assault centers are familiar with the complexities of child sexual abuse, often already collaborate with police, and frequently already work with the prosecuting attorneys.

PARENTS

Whereas victims can directly ensure that offenders do not continue to molest other children by reporting the offenders, parents can directly intervene by not providing Groomers with children to molest. Informed parents can render entire towns inhospitable to Groomer child molesters. The parents who absorb the information in this book, accept that no friend is automatically above suspicion, and recognize that those who fit the Groomer profile should not be left alone with children, will be able to better protect children. This does not mean everyone is a pedophile. This does not require parents to become vigilantes. It simply means parents can take direct responsibility for protecting children by not encouraging those whose motives are suspect. There is no harm in making sure that people fitting this profile are closely supervised. When Groomers feel too closely supervised and are not given easy access to children they quickly disappear, a confirmation that their motives may have been suspect. This is the first line of defense, but it is not the only prevention strategy available to parents.

Remember that child sexual abuse flourishes in secrecy and isolation. Any time that parents become suspicious, the solution to stopping any potential abuse is to break out of that framework. They cannot worry alone. They should not wonder by themselves. They should seek support and network with other parents and with professionals familiar with child sex abuse. This will allow them to learn if their worries are valid or whether they are overreacting. Earlier reporting must be established so that parents do not have to wait for blatantly obvious evidence of child sexual abuse before going to the police. When parents see troublesome behavior, they need to be able to discuss it with trained professionals to learn whether they are overreacting. At the same time, they must feel secure that such discussions do not needlessly point the finger at innocent individuals. Sexual assault centers, with trained professional staff, can provide a place to confidentially discuss information, where concerns can be put in perspective, and information can be carefully screened.

Parents trying to protect children from Groomers should be supported. Discussing their observations and worries with trained professionals will help them differentiate unnecessary anxieties from legitimately worrisome conduct. Talking to staff at a sexual assault clinic would not be too difficult. Many of the parents confused by Coach Carl, or those who decided to remove their children from further contact with Marvelous Marvin, never felt that they had sufficient cause to lodge an official police investigation. However, they felt uneasy with what they saw, and worried about the other children. Talking to staff at the local sexual assault clinic would have provided them with perspective, guidance, and support. Things were different in the community where Dr. Dan lived because of a sexual assault program that existed in the community. It operated like many of these programs, in which assault staff work closely with local police, prosecutors, and medical staff in their efforts to help facilitate reporting, as well as ease the victims' transition through the legal system. Because one of the mothers who had concerns about Dr. Dan's conduct worked at a sexual assault clinic, she was able to share the information she had with colleagues. Since there was no reported event that was actionable, nothing further was done in this case.

GROUPS, ORGANIZATIONS, AND OFFICIALS

Sexual Assault Clinics

Sexual assault clinics are crucial in supporting individuals, families, and organizations struggling with potential child molesters in their midst. Staff at sexual assault centers describe how they hear the same names come up again and again. They already are well trained in helping victims prepare for court. They understand the emotional complexities in testifying against an offender, but also know the pain caused by remaining silent and maintaining the victim's stance. They can help provide reality checks to parents who may not know whether their concerns are realistic or whether they are being overprotective. They can provide networking between families so that the information known to each family no longer remains isolated. They can contact the assault centers in other towns where the alleged offender has already lived and learn from their colleagues whether the individual created similar problems in these other communities. They can, with permission, help unite the various players to provide them with the knowledge and the support to report information to the police and to ensure that the police investigations incorporate all the possible information.

State Child Protection Agencies

State child protection agencies are often asked to make custody recommendations, sometimes inadvertently choosing the "slicker" adult without understanding the need for closer scrutiny. By the time that Businessman Bob's case to regain custody of his younger daughters went to court he looked like the calmer, more rational parent. All his successes at gaining access to the girls, and all his undermining of Wanda's attempts to protect them resulted in making Wanda look crazier and crazier. By the time the authorities became involved in making custody decisions, they saw a very calm, financially established man, and a very overwrought ex-wife with no money. They failed to understand the dynamics or the significance of his history. In fact, the evaluator that child protective services (CPS) first hired to assess both parents promoted the idea that children who had previously lived with Businessman Bob be contacted. This was, unfortunately, viewed as too cumbersome and time-consuming, and another evaluator was therefore used. Although an evaluator would not have the authority to conduct such an investigation, CPS would have such authority.

By understanding how the well-socialized child molester often operates, those responsible for doing evaluations will be less quick to believe these smooth talkers during custody cases, and more likely to investigate the case thoroughly. They will also be less quick to assume that a previous child molester has "turned over a new leaf" and can be trusted. They will also be sensitive to the nuances characteristic of Groomers, and thus be less easily led. Most important, they need to work together with the sexual assault centers. Staff in these centers can provide support, guidance, and perspective, in ensuring that more complete corroborating information is obtained since such staff already are on the front lines, and could therefore have access to relevant information. CPS also needs to work closely with trained forensic experts who are familiar with Groomers anytime sexual abuse allegations occur, collaborating effectively to ensure that they are not inadvertently giving custody to child molesters.

Law Enforcement

Police need to learn how to investigate these cases when allegations do arise. By understanding the well-socialized child molester, they will have a better idea of where to look for clues, and will understand everyone in a Groomer's life can potentially provide useful information. Knowing the modus operandi is crucial to running a good investigation. For instance, just as drug investigations are aided by talking to landlords who have significant clues about the activities that take place in the house, so do former girlfriends, family members, and others know about the molesters among them. The police need to know who to talk to, and how to ask the right questions, and then they need to listen carefully. They will also need to develop a greater ease with the topic to avoid making the mistakes police interviewing Marvelous Marvin made. The police also need to investigate cases even after an identified offender has already been convicted. All too often, once a conviction is obtained, the other evidence seems redundant and therefore fails to be included in any subsequent decisions. Once Bottom-feeder Buddy was convicted for Indecent Liberties, the police stopped talking to the other women whose children he had molested, "We got our guy. What's the point?" The problem is that when it comes to risk-assessment practices and release planning, *all* the evidence is crucial.

Prosecuting Attorneys

Prosecuting attorneys can be key gatekeepers in protecting the community. Often, prosecutors allow child molesters to plead down a sexually motivated crime, in the interest of saving taxpayers' dollars by quickly obtaining a guilty plea to a lesser charge in lieu of the expense to investigate. For instance, a rape can become a fourth-degree assault conviction, which no longer conveys the sexualized nature of the criminal activity. In the long-run, however, every pled-down conviction further masks the true behavior. The real cost to the public is much more expensive as child molesters continue to have free reign in the community. Many of Bottom-feeder Buddy's convictions were for assaults, which failed to accurately identify his sexually aggressive conduct toward minors.

Furthermore, if another sex offense occurs while the individual is on probation, it typically is identified as a probation violation, again masking the true nature of the crime, which impacts risk-assessment data. Such probation violations, which disappear from the criminal record, should be viewed as significant, important information in determining meaningful management strategies.

Prosecutors could also recommend more extensive investigations when child molester cases suggest the probability of other victims. Identifying earlier victims, should this exist, not only helps to strengthen the case, but also ensures the victims will be more easily supported. The compounded testimony of a number of victims becomes more powerful and effective in securing a conviction, and provides the victims further support and courage.

Organizations

The Groomers under discussion gravitate toward organizations where there are children. All organizations responsible for children need to develop protocols for correctly handling any complaints of inappropriate conduct that they receive. As already noted, parents talk to principals when they worry about a teacher's conduct. The parents who worried about Cranky Coach Carl went to the soccer league. When complaints are lodged, even if it would appear there is insufficient information to warrant an investigation, the decision making should be made by trained professionals. Organizations should never attempt internal investigations, both for their own protection as well as to protect the interests of the employee and the children. The soccer league should have had a protocol in place, and then when complaints were made about Cranky Coach Carl there would have been no appearance of any conflict of interest. Furthermore, any information regarding possible improprieties would have been referred to the investigating agency. The Catholic Church would have similarly benefited from immediately referring every complaint about pedophile priests to outside investigators.

Judges

Judges need to become educated about child sexual abuse and understand the dynamics of how child molesters operate and what information they need to make a reasonable determination. The judge who gave Businessman Bob custody of his three younger daughters, commenting that the girls could use locks on the bedroom doors to further ensure safety, demonstrated a failure to understand the dangers and problems inherent in child sexual abuse cases.

Departments of Corrections

Anywhere from 20 to 30 percent of prison beds are filled with convicted child molesters. Many of these offenders present few management problems while incarcerated, and benefit from treatment programs offered in the prison setting. However, behavioral habits developed in the closely structured setting of a prison do not translate into improved behavior on the "outside." Prison staff can and do help facilitate transitions back into the community, but they are neither funded nor legally mandated to continue to monitor child molesters, and often cannot supervise all risky behavior.

Sex Offender Treatment Programs

Sex offender treatment providers currently treat a number of offenders on an outpatient basis. Typically, those seen as most amenable for treatment receive the SSOSA option in lieu of prison. However, even convicted child molesters who do not initially qualify for SSOSA are still required to participate in therapy upon their release from prison. Presumably, those offenders who remain in treatment, much like the alcoholic who participates in a meaningful twelve-step program, present less community risk precisely because they have close ongoing supervision and accountability with professionals trained to recognize high-risk behavior.

Community Corrections Officers

Upon their return to the community, released child molesters typically have a period of mandated supervision. Community corrections officers need to become familiar with the specific details in every case they supervise to ensure that the people on their caseloads are refraining from further sexual misconduct. The information they need requires an awareness of how child molesters operate, a thorough understanding of the specific monitoring requirements in every case, in combination with close and careful collaboration with community members and sexual assault centers to ensure greater access to necessary feedback. Unfortunately, such supervision is usually time limited.

Researchers

Actuarial tools have provided a measurable guide, but fail to adequately incorporate corroborating data essential to better assessing ongoing risk. Current strategies need to be refined so that future approaches incorporate all the relevant clinical and corroborating data to develop actuarial guidelines that more meaningfully differentiate levels of risk among the socially skilled Groomers, which is crucial to developing management considerations, and monitoring behavior.

CUSTODY BATTLES

Accusations of child sexual abuse that occur in the context of a custody battle are often seen as bogus. One mother described divorcing her physically violent and abusive husband and having the courts grant her full custody with the ex-husband having only supervised visitations with his young daughter. Once the child learned of the new arrangement, she disclosed to the therapist that her father had also been sexually abusing her, which the therapist reported to the court as required. The courts at that point immediately decided the allegations were trumped up, reversed the earlier decision, and instead gave the father full custody with no contact allowed with the mother. By understanding the socially skilled Groomer, such errors can be avoided.

Although in some custody battles sudden charges of sexual abuse may be fraudulent, this is not true in every case. Reasonably, children who had refrained from telling when the offending parent still lived at home, will be more likely to disclose information about sexual abuse for the first time after that parent leaves the home.

Dr. Dan spent very little time with his wife, Mary. When his daughter became a teenager, he began to shower her with special presents and suddenly seemed very attentive to her. He took her on outings where it would typically be expected a husband would take his wife. When he went to professional development conferences, he suddenly showed an interest in having his beautiful young daughter come along. His wife Mary began worrying more and more about her husband's behavior with the young girl. Then, when her daughter was fourteen years old Mary unexpectedly became pregnant, and the couple had a son. Dr. Dan was ecstatic. Mary became increasingly morose as she worried about her husband's conduct, and felt isolated in the family. Suddenly, Dr. Dan demanded a divorce, and insisted he should have custody of both children, arguing that his wife's increasing depression made her unfit to be a mother.

Mary watched her world come tumbling down. She sought treatment and obtained legal advice. Her daughter began dropping hints about not wanting to live with her father, saying, "He's creepy. I don't like the way he kisses me." Mary began paying closer attention, worried about her daughter, and took her to see a therapist. In the course of treatment, the girl disclosed that her father had been trying to have sex with her. "He said I have to learn to do it the right way. He's a doctor so he can teach me stuff." When Mary told the lawyer she wanted full custody because of concerns regarding sexual misconduct, her lawyer said, "Forget it. You haven't got a chance." She was told to not even consider mentioning these events in the custody hearing or she would be in danger of losing all rights to have access to her children.

Had the courts been aware of Dr. Dan's almost continuous conduct, the parenting evaluation would have more reasonably reflected the danger he presented. Because no indications of sexual abuse ever arose prior to the custody hearing, however, the allegations would have been viewed by the authorities as a spiteful ploy by a vindictive wife in an attempt to get revenge against a very handsome and successful man. Any such allegations made by the daughter would have reflected "coaching" from Mary.

Mary was beside herself, and finally sought help at the local sexual assault center. In this particular community, as already noted, one of the staff had already personally experienced earlier difficulties with Dr. Dan's conduct toward her son. She became intrigued by Mary's situation. She called a number of mothers in the community with whom she had discussed earlier concerns about Dr. Dan. Each of the families talked more closely with their children and obtained detailed information. The families agreed to talk to one another and with the police. Many of their sons, who were now much older and no longer worried that disclosing what had been done to them would harm their status at school, also agreed to talk.

Staff at the sexual assault center helped the various participants understand the emotional and legal complexities that could be expected should they come forward. Family members and children talked to one another only after having given consent. After a number of meetings with sexual assault center staff, together with an investigating police officer, a full-scale investigation was launched. In this case, Mary retained custody of the children, Dr. Dan lost his medical license, and he was convicted on a number of counts of sexual assault against his daughter as well as against many of the boys in the community.

CONCLUSION

Child sexual abuse will not end without the full cooperation of all adults working together to keep children safe. To do so successfully requires that the information known to those in the community becomes available to those charged with the responsibility for managing risk. Information regarding all arrests and convictions for sexually motivated misconduct should be maintained on an international database so that those child molesters who choose to relocate in order to avoid the repercussions of their past conduct can continue to be successfully monitored.

Most important, child sexual abuse should be seen as a virus that flourishes in secrecy and isolation. The best treatment for inoculating communities and protecting children is open communication. There is no shame in being the target of a child molester. All families with children are constantly being targeted in that manner. The shame and embarrassment should be placed squarely on the shoulders of molesters. Community members who know what to look for can correctly help identify those whose sexual habits endanger children and should not be tolerated. Communities can then provide such individuals with the help and support needed to stop their misconduct, rather than providing continued access to children while praising their superficially winning ways. By protecting the innocent, everyone wins. The world becomes less safe for child molesters while those with honorable intentions need not fear being falsely accused.

References

Abel, G., Becker, J., Mittleman, M., Rouleau, J., & Murphy, W. (1987). Self-reported sex crimes of nonincarcerated paraphiliacs. *Journal of Interpersonal Violence, 2*(1), March.

Abel, G., Rouleau, J., & Cunningham-Rathner, J. (1986). Sexually aggressive behavior. In W. Curran, A.L. McGarry, and S.A. Shah (Eds.), *Forensic psychiatry and psychology: Perspectives and standards for interdisciplinary practice* (pp. 289-313). Phildadelphia: F.A. Davis Company.

Alexander, M.A. (1999). Sexual offender treatment efficacy revisited. *Sexual Abuse: A Journal of Research and Treatment, 11*(2), 101-115.

American Psychiatric Association (2000). *Diagnostic and statistical manual of mental disorders* (Fourth edition - Text revision.). Washington, DC: Author.

Barbaree, H. (1997). Evaluating treatment efficacy with sexual offenders: The insensitivity of recidivism studies to treatment effects. *Sexual Abuse: A Journal of Research and Treatment, 9*(2), 111-128.

Bolen, R.M. (2001). *Child sexual abuse: Its scope and our failure.* New York: Kluwer Academic/Plenum Publishers.

Brongersma, E. (1991). Boy-lovers and their influence on boys: Distorted research and anecdotal observations. *Journal of Homosexuality 20*(1/2), 145-173.

Carnes, P. (1983). *The sexual addiction.* Minneapolis: CompCare Publications.

Carnes, P.J. (1996). Addiction or compulsion: Politics or illness. *Journal of Sexual Addiction and Compulsivity, 3,* 127-149.

Committee for Children (2001). Talk about touching: A personal safety curriculum. Seattle, WA: Author.

Cook, G. (1989). *Grooming male children: A brief overview.* Unpublished document.

de Becker, G. (1999). *Protecting the gift: Keeping children and teenagers safe from violence.* New York: Little Brown and Company.

Doren, D.M. (1998). Recidivism base rates, predictions of child molester recidivism, and the "sexual predator" commitment laws. *Behavioral Sciences and the Law, 16,* 97-114.

Doren, D.M. (2002). *Evaluating child molesters: A manual for civil commitments and beyond.* Thousand Oaks, CA: Sage Publications.

Epperson, D.L., Kaul, J.D., & Huot, S.J. (1995). *Predicting risk of recidivism for incarcerated child molesters: Updated development of the Minnesota Child Molester Screening Tool (MnSost).* Paper presented at the fourteenth annual research and treatment conference of the Association for Sexual Abusers, New Orleans, November.

Festinger, L. (1957). *A theory of cognitive dissonance.* Evanston, IL: Row, Peterson.

Finkelhor, D. (1983). Removing the child—prosecuting the offender in cases of child sexual abuse: Evidence from the national reporting system for child abuse and neglect. *Child Abuse & Neglect, 7,* 195-205.

Flora, R. (2001). *How to work with child molesters: A handbook for criminal justice, human service, and mental health professionals.* Binghamton, NY: The Haworth Press.

Gilligan, C. (1992). *In a different voice: Psychological theory and women's development.* Boston: Harvard University Press.

Greenberg, D.M. (1998). Sexual recidivism in child molesters. *Canadian Journal of Psychiatry, 43,* June, 459-465.

Halliday-Sumner, L. (1997). *Sexual abuse: Disclosures.* Courtenay, British Columbia: Lalyn Publications.

Hanson, R.K. (1998). What do we know about child molester risk assessment? *Psychology, Public Policy, and Law, 4*(172), 50-72.

Hanson, R.K. & Bussiere, M.T. (1998). Predicting relapse: A meta-analysis of sexual offender recidivism studies. *Journal of Consulting and Clinical Psychology, 66*(2), 348-362.

Hanson, R.K., Harrris, A., Gray, G.A., Forouzan, E., McWhinnie, A.J., & Osweiler, M.C. (1997, October). *Dynamic predictors of sexual reoffense project 1997.* Presentation to the sixteenth annual research and treatment conference of the Association for the Treatment of Sexual Abusers, Arlington, Virginia.

Hare, R.D. (1991). *The Hare psychopathy checklist–rev. manual.* Toronto: Multi-Health Systems, Inc.

Klassen, D. & O'Connor, W.A. (1994). Demographic and case history variables in risk assessment. In J. Monahan & H.J. Steadman (Eds.), *Violence and mental disorder: Developments in risk assessment* (pp. 229-258). Chicago: University of Chicago Press.

Kübler-Ross, E. (1969). *On death and dying: What the dying have to teach doctors, nurses, clergy, and their own family.* New York: Touchstone Press.

Litwack, T.R. (2001). Actuarial versus clinical assessments of dangerousness. *Psychology, Public Policy, and Law, 7*(2), 409-443.

Looman, J., Abracen, J., & Nicholaichuk, T.P. (2000). Recidivism among treated sexual offenders and matched controls. *Journal of Interpersonal Violence, 15*(3), 279-290.

Marques, J.K., Day, D.M., Nelson, C., & West, M.A. (1994). Effects of cognitive behavioral treatment on child molester recidivism. *Criminal Justice and Behavior, 21*(1), March, 28-54.

Masterson, J.F. (1988). *The search for the real self: Unmasking the personality disorders of our age.* New York: Free Press.

Millon, T., Simonsen, E., Birket-Smith, M., & Davis, R.D. (1998). *Psychopathy: Antisocial, criminal, and violent behavior.* New York: The Guilford Press.

Monahan, J. (1981). *Predicting violent behavior: An assessment of clinical techniques.* Beverly Hills, CA: Sage.

Pipher, M. (1996). *The shelter of each other: Rebuilding our families.* New York: Ballantine Books.

Prochaska, J.O., Norcross, J.C., & Diclemente, C.C. (1994). *Changing for good: A revolutionary six-stage program for overcoming bad habits and moving your life positively forward.* New York: Avon Books.

Quinsey, V.L., Harris, G.T., Rice, M.E., & Cormier, C.A. (1998). *Violent offenders: Appraising and managing risk.* Washington, DC: American Psychological Association.

Quinsey, V.L., Lalumiere, M.L., Rice, M.E., & Harris, G.T. (1995). Predicting sexual offenses. In J.C. Campbell (Ed.), *Assessing dangerousness: Violence by sexual offenders, batterers, and child abusers* (pp. 114-137). Thousand Oaks, CA: Sage.

Rush, F. (1980). *The best kept secret: Sexual abuse of children.* New York: McGraw-Hill Book Company.

Salter, A.C. (1995). *Transforming trauma: A guide to understanding and treating adult survivors of child sexual abuse.* Thousand Oaks, CA: Sage Publications.

Salter, A.C. (2003). *Predators, pedophiles, rapists, and other child molesters: Who they are, how they operate, and how we can protect ourselves, and our children.* New York: Basic Books.

Sauzier, M. (1989). Disclosure of child sexual abuse: For better or for worse. *Psychiatric Clinics of North America, 12*(2), 445-469.

Schlank, A. & Cohen, F. (1999). *The sexual predator: Law, policy, evaluation, and treatment.* Kingston, NJ: Civic Research Institute.

Schlank, A. & Cohen, F. (2001). *The sexual predator: Legal issues, clinical issues, special populations.* Kingston, NJ: Civic Research Institute.

Seto, M.C. & Barbaree, H.E. (1999). Psychopathy, treatment behavior, and child molester recidivism. *Journal of Interpersonal Violence,* December, 1235-1247.

Silva, D.C. (1990). Pedophilia: An autobiography. In J.R. Feierman (Ed.), *Pedophilia: Biosocial dimensions.* New York: Springer-Verlag.

Summit, R. (1989). The centrality of victimization: Regaining the focal point of recovery for survivors of child sexual abuse. *Psychiatric Clinics of North America, 12*(2), June, 413-430.

The Investigative Staff of *The Boston Globe* (2002). *Betrayal: The crisis in the Catholic Church.* Boston: Little Brown and Company.

Tjaden, P.G. & Thoennes, N. (1992). Predictors of legal intervention in child maltreatment cases. *Child Abuse & Neglect, 16,* 807-821.

van Dam, C. (1996). *How child sexual molesters groom adults to gain access to children.* Doctoral dissertation. Cincinnati, Ohio: The Union Institute.

van Dam, C. (2001). *Identifying child molesters: Preventing child sexual abuse by recognizing the patterns of the offenders.* Binghamton, NY: The Haworth Press.

van Dam, C., Halliday, L., & Bates, C. (1985). The occurrence of sexual abuse in a small community. *Canadian Journal of Community Mental Health, 4*(1), 105-111.

Webster, C.D., Harris, G.T., Rice, M.E., Cormier, C., & Quinsey, V.L. (1994). *The violence prediction scheme: Assessing dangerousness in high risk men.* Toronto: University of Toronto, Centre of Criminology.

Willmsen, C. & O'Hagan, M. (2003, December 14). Coaches who prey: The abuse of girls and the system that allows it. *The Seattle Times,* p. 1.

Zeeck, D.A. (2003, December 19). State, schools can do more to protect girls from predators. *The News Tribune,* p. B-6.

Index

Access, 2
Accidents, as explanations, 55
Actuarial approach
    grabbers, 119
    risk assessment, 116-117, 125
Actuarial data
    base rate, 120-121
    recidivism rates, 118-119
Actuarial scales
    limitations of, 132
    risk assessment, 125-126
    risk factors, 126-131
Addiction
    child molesters, 59-60, 137
    sexual, 1-2
Adolescent girls, poor judgement,
        53-54
Adolescents, consensual behavior,
        66-68
Adults
    boundary violations, 47
    charm of groomer, 2, 3, 47
    as enablers, 3-4
    molester's view of, 1, 3
    observing minor offenses, 31, 88
    protection strategies, 33
Age
    child sexual abuse, 48
    consensual sex, 59
    legal consent, 69
    as risk factor, 130
Alcohol use
    DWI convictions, 119-120
    as explanation, 56
Allegations to police, level five
        investigation, 96-97
Alzheimer's disease, Predictable Peter,
        62-63

Amber Alert System, use of, 39
America's Most Wanted, 39
Antisocial Personality disorder, 129
Arrest
    level six-nine investigation, 100
    and recidivism, 118
Attention, interviews, 105
Attentiveness, 104

Baby sitting, case example, 16
Bad touch, self-protection lessons,
        35-36
Base rates, sexual assault data, 120-121
"Big Brother," 24
Bob. *See* Businessman Bob
Bottom-feeder Buddy
    antisocial behavior, 129
    case example, 27-29, 31, 32
    as future risk, 114
    level III offender, 115
    level five investigation, 97
    level six-nine investigation, 100,
        101
    level three investigation, 91
    misdemeanor charges, 38
    police response, 143
    prosecution of, 144
Boundary violations, 3-4, 9-10
Boys
    offender target, 42
    risk factors, 131-132
Buddy. *See* Bottom-feeder Buddy
Businessman Bob
    age factor, 130
    case example, 10-14, 31, 32
    conviction of, 98
    corroborating data, 122, 123